Painting in Tongues

Organized by Michael Darling

Essays by Michael Darling and Friedrich Wolfram Heubach

The Museum of Contemporary Art, Los Angeles

This publication accompanies
the exhibition "Painting in Tongues,"
organized by Michael Darling and
presented at The Museum of Contemporary Art,
Los Angeles, 29 January—17 April 2006.

"Painting in Tongues" is made possible by
generous support from the MOCA Contemporaries,
the Frederick R. Weisman Art Foundation,
Martin and Rebecca Eisenberg Foundation,
and Beth Swofford.
In-kind support is provided
by the Goethe-Institut.
Promotional support is provided by
KJAZZ 88.1FM.

Director of Publications: Lisa Mark
Senior Editor: Jane Hyun
Editor: Elizabeth Hamilton
Administrative Assistant: Theeng Kok
Designer: Willem Henri Lucas
Printer: Graphicom, Vicenza, Italy

ISBN 0-914357-94-8

Printed and bound in Graphicom, Vicenza, Italy

CONTENTS

FOREWORD

"Painting in Tongues" presents the work of seven artists who address the complexity of contemporary life through a single timeless medium: paint. As the title suggests, their individual bodies of work communicate through a range of visual languages and techniques, distinct voices rather then a single identifiable signature style. In showcasing these leading young artists of today, "Painting in Tongues" attempts to reflect upon the origins of painting and to suggest where it might go in the future. Of course, painting has refused to die or be condemned to irrelevancy; in recent years, in fact, it has enjoyed renewed interest in art schools, artist studios, the press, and the marketplace. For his first group exhibition at The Museum of Contemporary Art, Los Angeles (MOCA), exhibition curator Michael Darling has chosen to highlight an artistic mode that seems to resist definition or categorization and, in so doing, opens up new critical terrain.

One important function the museum serves involves putting new artistic movements and innovations into context. "Painting in Tongues" joins MOCA's distinguished history of presenting exhibitions that mark significant tendencies in contemporary art, including "A Forest of Signs: Art in the Crisis of Representation" (1989), organized by Ann Goldstein; "Ecstasy: In and About Altered States" (2005) and "Helter Skelter: L.A. Art in the 1990s" (1992), organized by Paul Schimmel; and "Afterimage: Drawing Through Process" (1999) and "Flight Patterns" (2002), organized by Connie Butler. In addition, "Painting in Tongues" brings the work of artists from Germany and the United Kingdom to Los Angeles, while also highlighting the work of three Southern California artists. In this way, the exhibition suggests concerns that are not specific to one locale but underlie a broader re-interrogation of painting.

Exhibitions such as "Painting in Tongues" require the support of many. I am deeply grateful to MOCA's Board of Trustees for standing behind this exhibition. In addition, I would like to thank its visionary funders: the MOCA Contemporaries, the Frederick R. Weisman Art Foundation, the Martin and Rebecca Eisenberg Foundation, and Beth Swofford. We are also indebted to the artists—Kai Althoff, Gillian Carnegie, Mark Grotjahn, Lucy McKenzie, Rodney McMillian, Ivan Morley, and Anselm Reyle—for their commitment to this presentation.

Jeremy Strick
Director

ACKNOWLEDGMENTS

The organization of this exhibition at The Museum of Contemporary Art, Los Angeles (MOCA), has been a joy from the beginning, as I have not only had the opportunity to work closely with a fantastic group of artists, but also benefited from a large network of supportive colleagues. I am particularly indebted to MOCA Director Jeremy Strick and Chief Curator Paul Schimmel for their faith in the exhibition and commitment to seeing it through. The lenders to the exhibition also deserve great thanks for parting with their treasured objects, and for that I am grateful to Kai Althoff; Gillian Carnegie; Wendy Chang; Rena Conti and Ivan Moskowitz; the Cranford Collection; Rosa and Carlos de la Cruz; Martin and Rebecca Eisenberg; Gerald Fineberg; Mark Grotjahn; Gustavo Hernandez; David and Tia Hoberman; The Institute of Contemporary Art, Boston; Matthew Kozol; Kourosh Larizadeh and Luis Pardo; Lucy McKenzie; The Museum of Modern Art, New York; the Ovitz Family Collection; Gregory Papadimitriou; Craig Robins; Gaby and Wilhelm Schürmann; Sam and Shanit Schwartz; Sarah Staton; Beth Swofford; David Teiger; Mario Testino; Dean Valentine and Amy Adelson; Joel Wachs; Dianne Wallace; Sylvie Winckler; and a number of private collectors.

Crucial help of another sort was provided by the generous funders of the exhibition, starting with the large grant from the MOCA Contemporaries as well as commitments from the Frederick R. Weisman Art Foundation, the Martin and Rebecca Eisenberg Foundation, and Beth Swofford. The Goethe-Institut also extended much appreciated support to the project, as did KJAZZ 88.1FM.

In developing the exhibition and assembling the list of artists, I relied on a wide network of friends and acquaintances with knowledge of great painting being made around the globe. Midori Matsui was an early sounding-board for the show, helping me to hone the conceptual underpinnings of the project and making protean contributions to my catalogue essay. Other confidants included Stephan Adamski, Ciléne Andréhn, Guido Baudach, Nicholas Baume, Tim Blum, Daniel Buchholz, Diedrich Diederichsen, Russell Ferguson, Marc Foxx, Ken Freed, Ann Goldstein, Rodney Hill, Dan Hug, Rita Kersting, Michael Krebber, Kourosh Larizadeh, Lars Bang Larsen, Chus Martinez, Martin McGeown, Dominic Molon, Charlotte Moser, Ivan Moskowitz, Christopher Muller, Christian Nagel, Giti Nourbakhsch, Jeff Poe, Jenelle Porter, Conny Purtill, Wilhelm Schürmann, Theo Tegelaers, Susanne Titz, Dean Valentine, Hamza Walker, and Barbara Weiss. Additional assistance by the artists' galleries was provided by Laura Mackall and Andrea Rosen at Andrea Rosen Gallery; Alexander Schröder and Scott Weaver at Galerie Neu; Anton Kern and Michael Clifton at Anton Kern Gallery; Gavin Brown, Corinna Durland, and Jaime Gecker at GBE Modern; Martin McGeown at Cabinet; Gisela Capitain and Regina Fiorito at Galerie Gisela Capitain; Giti Nourbakhsch and Sandra Bürgel at Galerie Giti Nourbakhsch; Sachi Yoshimoto at Patrick Painter, Inc.; Anja Dorn and Florian Baron at Galerie Christian Nagel; Susanne Vielmetter at Susanne Vielmetter Los Angeles Projects; and Helene Winer at Metro Pictures. MOCA Curatorial Associate Rebecca Morse also helped keep the exhibition on track in innumerable ways.

I was very fortunate to have met graphic designer Willem Henri Lucas, who is responsible for the stunning and smart design of this catalogue and was a pleasure to collaborate with. I was also very happy to have been guided by Diedrich Diederichsen to the brilliance of Friedrich Wolfram Heubach, whose contribution to the book expands upon and challenges the presuppositions of the exhibition. Translation of Professor Heubach's text was capably handled by James Gussen, while earlier translation assistance was provided by Leslie Weissgerber. The contents were also profoundly shaped by the sharp editorial guidance of MOCA Director of Publications Lisa Mark, along with the careful eyes of Jane Hyun, Elizabeth Hamilton, and Theeng Kok.

The exhibition was made possible not only by the artists and lenders but those who got the works to the museum, put them on the walls, and helped pay the bills. Director of Collections and Registration Robert Hollister handled a long and complicated list of shipping needs, while Director of Exhibition Production Brian Gray and his staff of Jang Park, Sebastian Clough, David Bradshaw, Shinichi Kitahara, Barry Grady, Monica Gonzalez, Jason Pugh, and Annabelle Medina carefully oversaw the installation. Educational programs established by Suzanne Isken, Aandrea Stang, and Catherine Arias added to the outreach of the exhibition. Fundraising was energetically spearheaded by Development Director Thom Rhue, Manager of Institutional Giving Jennifer Arceneaux, Manager of Individual Giving Laurie McGahey, and former Grants Writer Karen Lofgren. I am also grateful to Chief Financial Officer Jack Wiant for his beneficent protection of the overall budget.

Finally, I would like to thank my family for allowing me the time to travel and think, and the artists—Kai Althoff, Gillian Carnegie, Mark Grotjahn, Lucy McKenzie, Rodney McMillian, Ivan Morley, and Anselm Reyle—for challenging and expanding my notions of what painting can be.

Michael Darling

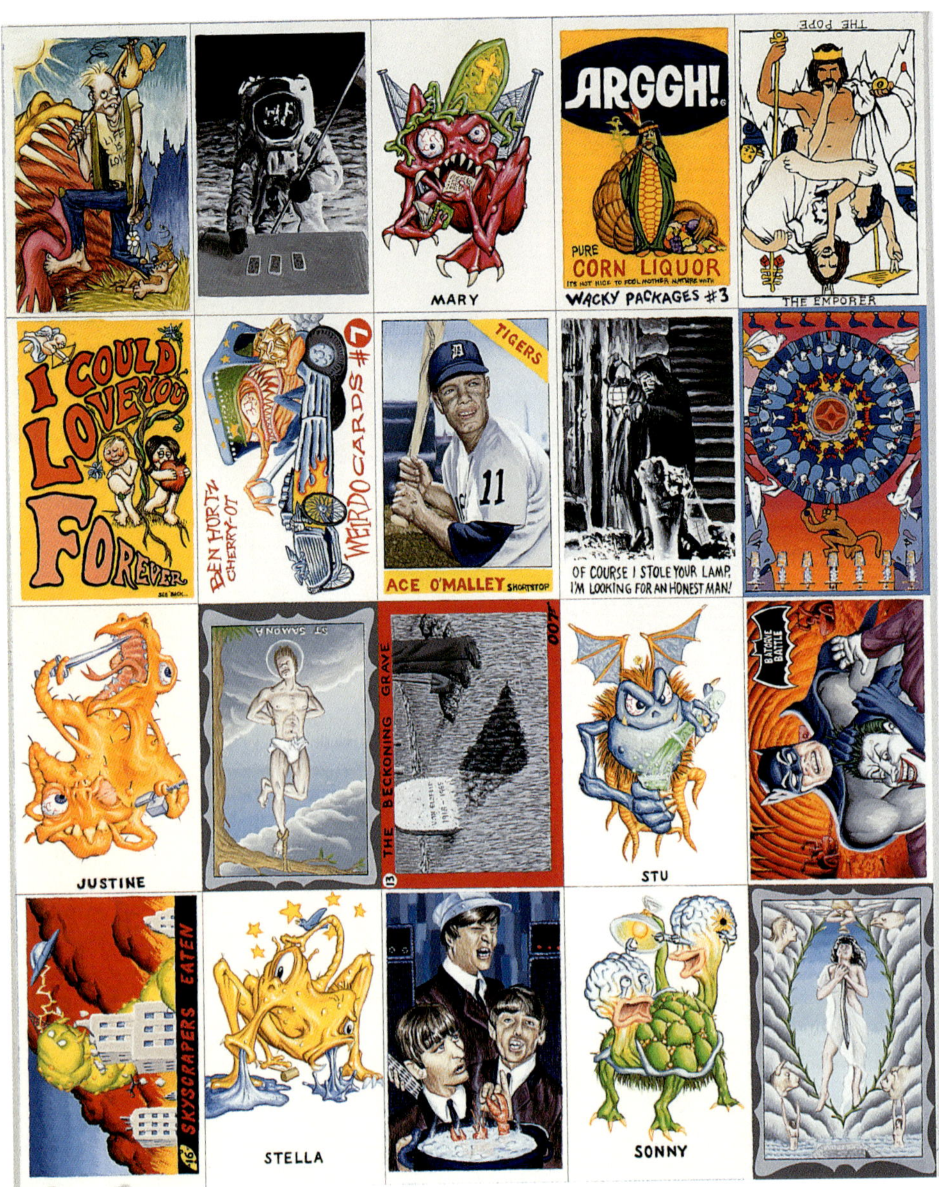

Jim Shaw
BUBBLE GUM CARDS (FRONTS), 1990, gouache on board, 17 x 14 inches
Collection of Linda and Jerry Janger, Los Angeles

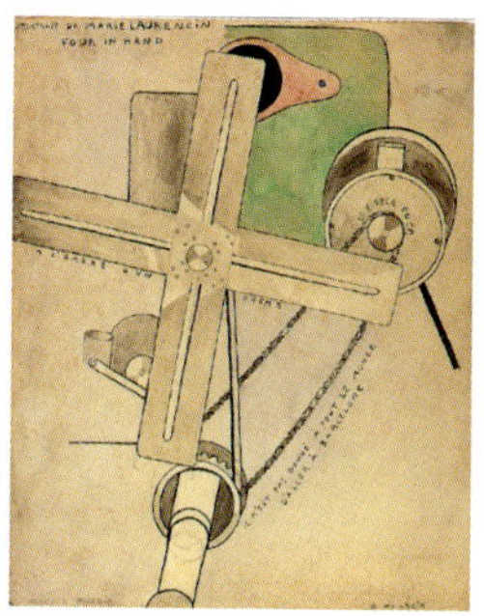
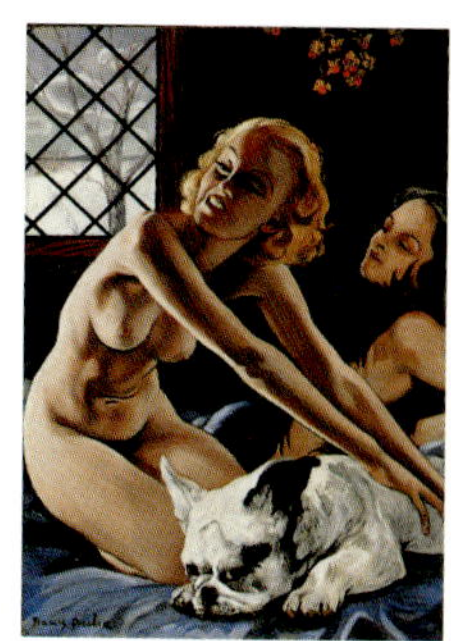

History seems most comfortably articulated through well-defined narratives, steady advances of plot, and regularly occurring flashes of clarity or resolution. Its linear cause-and-effect relationships are most persuasive when they can exist in and be nurtured by these conditions. Murky, complicated, backtracking storylines distract those attempting to forge master narratives but, in reality, they are essential to pushing culture forward. The history of modern art (despite its basis in the rebellious myths of the avant-garde) is also prone to "epic logic"[1]—that is, it tends to pursue the general through the specific to form causal relationships.

This syncretic and superficially compelling structure generally shows several careers cohering into a movement, and that movement begetting another movement, until one big fascinating march of time can be visualized. Generalizing histories of this kind tend to box artists into specific contemporaneous categories, downplaying or even eliding work that doesn't fit. Francis Picabia is a classic example of such inconsistency, someone whose mechanomorphic work from 1913 to 1922 made him a reliable and iconic platoon member of the then-emerging Dadaist movement, but whose later work was often dismissed by art historians and critics because of its seemingly anti-modernist turn toward realism and even kitsch.[2] (In an ironic turn, his work from the 1930s until his death in 1953 has only recently become appreciated precisely because of its provocative lack of coherence and its contempt for doctrinaire modernism.)

Within modernism, clarity was seen as a function of originality, an indication that one was true to oneself and one's time. However, originality has also been linked with the pursuit of a signature style, which would guarantee the artist his or her own self-defined wrinkle in the fabric of history. Over the last century, artists such as Picabia have forfeited the articulation of a single signature style in favor of a promiscuous pluralism, complicating their reception by their own milieu as well as the canon.

What is surprising is how deeply entrenched ideas of unity, singularity, and genius are in our society when there has been a considerable amount of theoretical work done to dismantle them over the past several decades. The artistic process itself could be said to be fundamentally at odds with such thinking. Indeed, as the theorist Anton Ehrenzweig described avant-garde practices in his 1967 book The Hidden Order of Art: "All artistic structure is essentially 'polyphonic'; it evolves not in a single line of thought, but in several superimposed strands at once. Hence creativity requires a diffuse, scattered kind of attention that contradicts our normal logical habits of thinking."[3] Ehrenzweig felt that the disorder found in much modern visual art—whether one was speaking of the pointillism

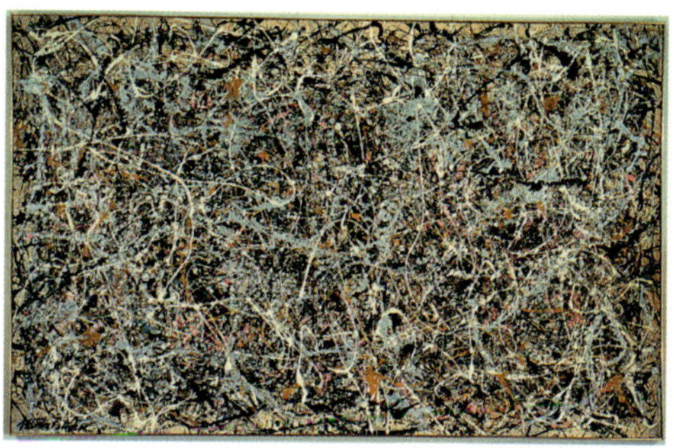

of Georges Seurat, the Cubism of Pablo Picasso, or the expressionism of
Jackson Pollock—could be seen as an attempt to subvert the totalizing
impulses of gestalt theories in order to allow for a more nuanced "hidden
order"[4] to emerge. The chaotic, for Ehrenzweig, was a much more fertile
space to work within: "The gestalt law of 'closure' ruling our surface
vision will always strive to round it off and polish its structure pre-
maturely and so may cut off its further development."[5]

This was hinted at even earlier by Walter Benjamin, whose influential
essay "One-Way Street" (1923–26) was similarly crystalline, built up of what
seemed to be a multitude of seemingly discrete voices, one of which intoned:
"To great writers, finished works weigh lighter than those fragments on
which they work throughout their lives. For only the more feeble and dis-
tracted take an inimitable pleasure in closure...'Genius is application.'"[6]

Much art of the last hundred years has incorporated the inconclusive
or the oppositional, in part as a distancing strategy to allow the discourse of art to develop beyond biography and mastery to include other
ideas and theories. A provisional history of this development might lead
from the Dadaist and Surrealist interest in chance, the tip of a wedge
that has steadily broken art-making away from its traditional bond with
mastery and craft while boldly favoring the laws of physics, mathematics,
or nature over the gilded hand of the trained genius.

Jackson Pollock, NUMBER 1, 1949, enamel and metallic paint on canvas, 63 x 102 inches
The Museum of Contemporary Art, Los Angeles. The Rita and Taft Schreiber Collection. Given
in loving memory of her husband, Taft Schreiber, by Rita Schreiber

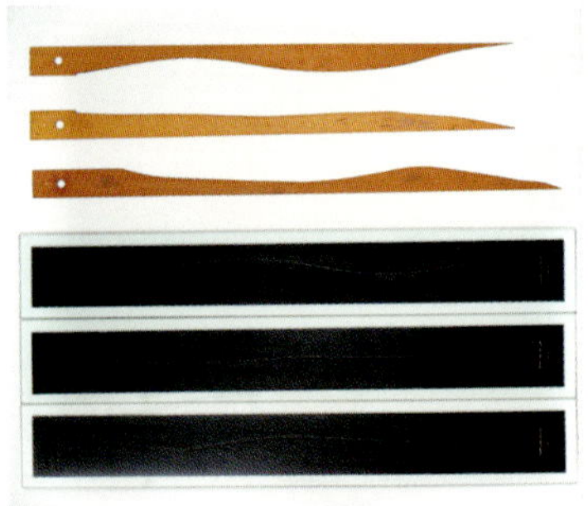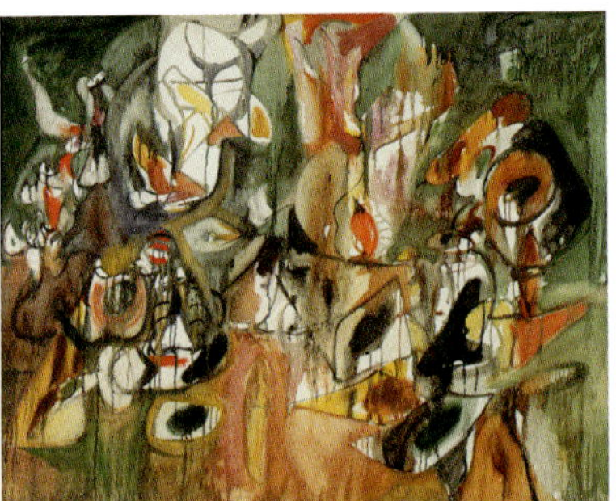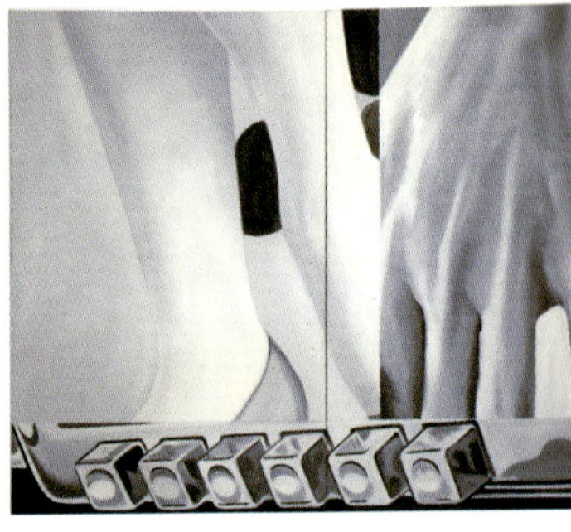

From Marcel Duchamp's Three Standard Stoppages (1913–14) to Arshile Gorky's thinned-out pours of paint, manipulating chance or accident and tapping into the unconscious mind signified a new paradigm in which the artist relinquished some degree of control. The Pop interest in commercial art—whether it was James Rosenquist's penchant for the anonymous and ubiquitous look of billboard painting, or Andy Warhol's and Roy Lichtenstein's adoption of the flat-screened appearance of ads and comics—likewise subverted the notion of the artist as the sole originator of the work. Conceptualists such as Sol LeWitt and Lawrence Weiner took this notion one step further, leaving the physical creation of artworks to others through written instructions. Others, such as Elaine Sturtevant and Richard Pettibone, mimicked the work of their peers to channel a more general temperature-taking of the aesthetic currency that dominated a particular time and place.

Though it is rife with experimentation, the recent history of painting has also been affected by the demands of the marketplace, where homogeneity and the fetishization of facture (the artist's direct touch) are seen as desirable. One artist who allowed the periodic tantalization of the brush but had the audacity to challenge his public's presumed desire for a coherent connection between paintings is Gerhard Richter. In the early 1960s, he had already exhibited a tendency toward variety, as is evident when comparing works such as Coffin Bearers (1962), Stag (1963), and

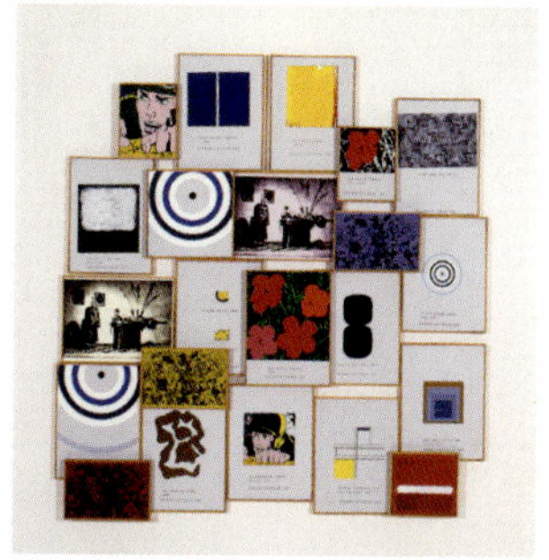 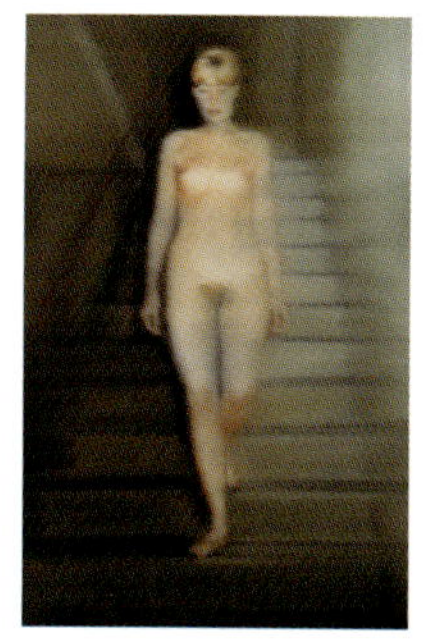 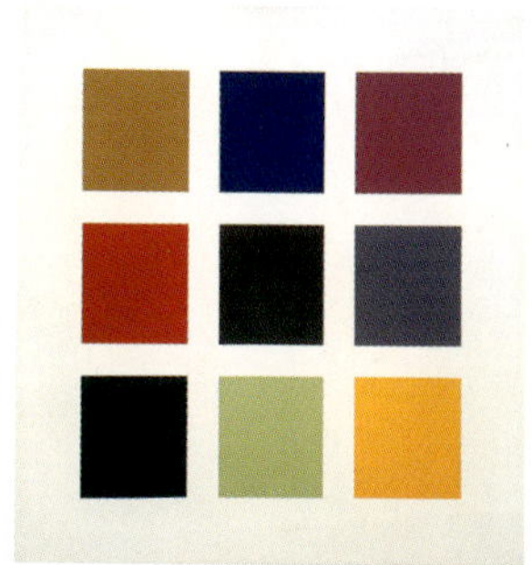

Dead (1963). By 1966, his attack on the notion of singular style was firmly established, as seen in Ema (Akt auf einer Treppe) (1966) and Farbtafel (1966–78).

Richter's career development has ricocheted between styles and genres, challenging the validity of categories such as abstraction and representation while putting forward a more unbounded vision of painting:

I pursue no objectives, no system, no tendency; I have no programme, no style, no direction. I have no time for specialized concerns, working themes, or variations that lead to mastery. I steer clear of definitions. I don't know what I want. I am inconsistent, non-committal, passive; I like the indefinite, the boundless; I like continual uncertainty. Other qualities may be conducive to achievement, publicity, success; but they are all outworn—as outworn as ideologies, opinions, concepts and names for things.[7]

While his example has given other artists license to rove freely among the myriad possibilities of painting, the sheer ambition of his project has ignored very few of the major and minor avenues of painterly practice, claiming as his own an intimidating number of modes.

Richter's peer Sigmar Polke presents another example of an artist establishing a legacy of painterly heterogeneity, albeit of a much less methodical nature. Polke's work is characterized less by its conquering

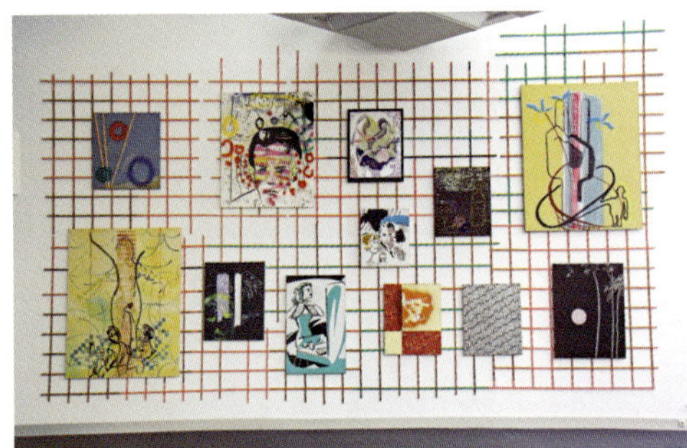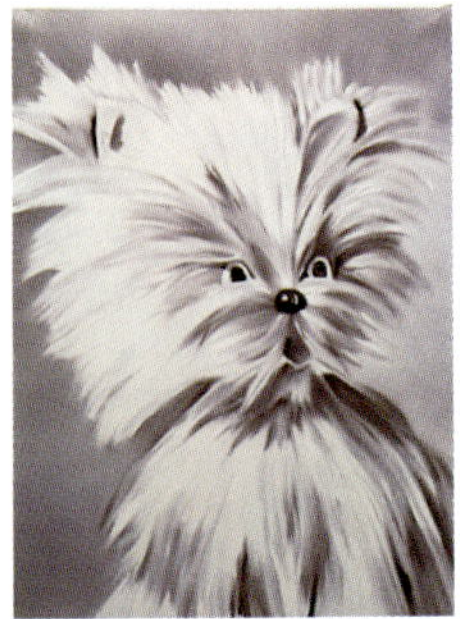

of categories than by its sustained quixotism, which was evident by the early 1960s, when he began employing a kaleidoscopic range of styles and subjects, often borrowing from advertising and sign painting. Within a few more years, his practice encompassed abstraction as well as all manner of representational modes—from the clumsy and naïve to the hyperrealistic. His multipanel piece Die 50er Jahre (1963–69), for example, maps a wide territory of visual phenomena and possibilities across twelve canvases.

One of the most distinctive qualities of Polke's work at this early stage was his incorporation of found printed fabrics, a feature that has remained constant in his work for forty years. These fabrics—whose patterns span the geometric and the floral, the exotic and the banal— introduce further extra-authorial elements that make plain the work's connection to the outside world. Polke's work has remained remarkably inquisitive and diverse in its formal inventiveness over the past four decades.

With Richter and Polke, Germany established itself as an important testing ground for the expansion of painterly language, a reputation that was extended by a second generation that includes Martin Kippenberger and Albert Oehlen. Kippenberger's oeuvre as a whole is wildly diverse and has set an influential example for many younger artists in

Sigmar Polke, DIE 50ER JAHRE (The fifties), 1963–69, mixed media on canvas, twelve canvases, dimensions variable
Hessisches Landesmuseum Darmstadt

Martin Kippenberger, HUND (Dog), 1981, acrylic on canvas, 78 3/4 x 59 1/16 inches
Collection of Albert Oehlen

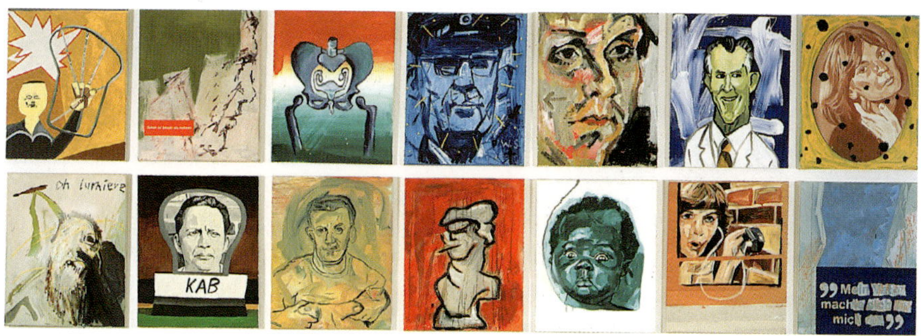

its humanistic embrace of often conflicting impulses and ideas. For instance, a work comprising twelve paintings executed by a sign painter named Werner on the occasion of Kippenberger's first museum show in Berlin, Lieber Maler, male mir (1981) reads as an abdication of artistic responsibility, an affront to cherished notions of authorship. Further complicating Kippenberger's authorial voice in this series is the sheer variety of the images, which include blurry black-and-white pornography, jewel-toned photorealism, logo-laden Pop, and in-your-face kitsch. Such variety was described by Anke Kempkes as "pictorial tourism."[8]

The later work Jeder ist seines Glückes Schmied (1983) also exemplifies this peripatetic approach to subject and style, presenting the viewer with a grid of equally sized canvases that contain such a cacophony of imagery and sources that scanning them is akin to flipping TV channels. This kind of visual polyphony was orchestrated in numerous other multi-canvas compositions around this period, each provocatively denying a sole authorial voice and admitting a failure to follow a single clear path of action. Putting this approach into context, the artist Lucy McKenzie wrote: "It's common for artists to use a specific language and set of references and images as shorthand in their work—a small lexicon of signs and subjects—but this only seems to achieve success when it becomes narrow to the point of extremity. A scaled-down version

Martin Kippenberger, detail of JEDER IST SEINES GLÜCKES SCHMIED (Every man is the architect of his own fortune), 1983, oil on canvas, twenty-one parts, 29 1/2 x 25 9/16 inches each Collection of Gaby and Wilhelm Schürmann, Aachen, Germany

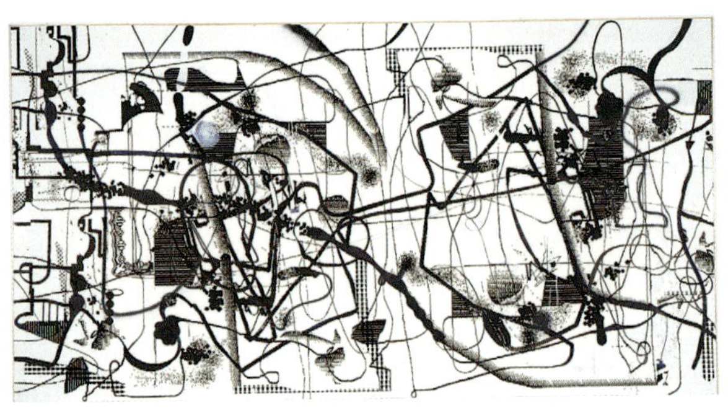

of Kippenberger's brand of quality control cannot help but seem lacking. The shotgun needs to be sawn-off to do the job properly."[9]

Kippenberger's close friend and peer Oehlen can also be counted as an important agitator in the fight against a single recognizable style. His work from the early 1980s to the present has been especially meaningful for its incorporation of a wide range of mark-making and painterly styles that complicate an easy reckoning of his "development." Indeed, as Timothy Martin wrote, Oehlen's practice militates against "<u>looking ahead</u> at the same time it frees it to <u>look around</u>,"[10] a subtle idea that nevertheless has huge implications for younger generations of painters. According to Martin, Oehlen's nonlinear expansion of his oeuvre is reliant on the concept of <u>détournement</u>, which "demands a split perspective of inside and outside language that is not ordered, and certainly not governed, on a principle of mirroring, of exclusive return to the social real, but on one of trespass and deterritorialization of formal and real realms. It loses and finds, locates and dislocates, as it churns through its source material."[11] Martin spoke about the counterbalancing of the artist's active, forceful, and controlling "<u>alpha</u> hand" with a "<u>beta</u> hand" that can be seen as an "agent of complexity (dare we call it negative entropy?)"[12] This is especially evident in Oehlen's computer paintings of the early 1990s that feature dueling

Albert Oehlen, UNTITLED, 1994, silkscreen print and acrylic paint on canvas, edition 14 of 94, 110 1/4 x 204 3/4 inches
Collection Taschen

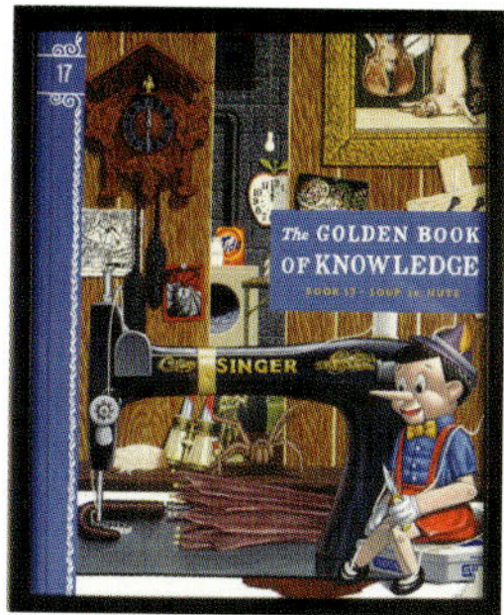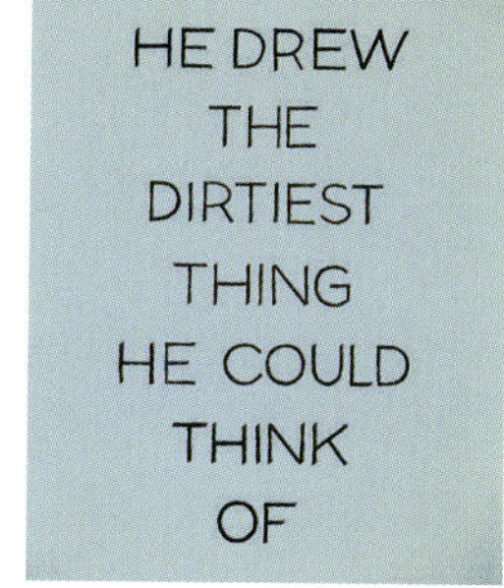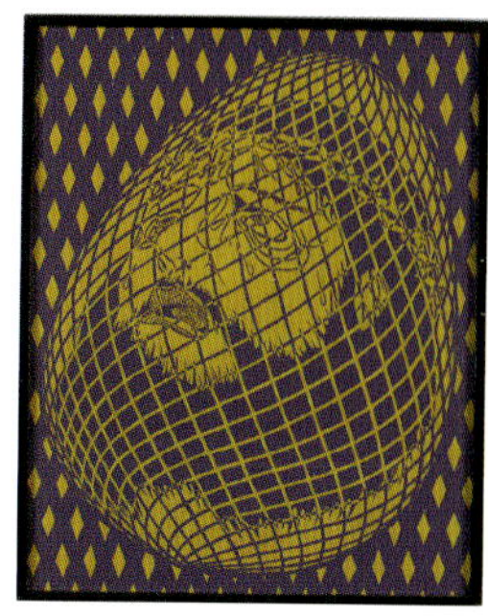

"hands" entwined, pushing authorship to the brink of anonymity.

Embracing the anonymous has been a key strategy in the subversion of painterly authorship. Although he is not frequently mentioned in the same context as his German counterparts, American artist Jim Shaw has made crucial contributions in this area. Much of his work is wrapped up in addressing his own historical, personal, and psychic minutiae; however, Shaw has also used himself as a medium through which the oddities of the visual world can be catalogued and observed. Two bodies of work in particular stand out for their direct relation to painting: My Mirage (1986–91) and Thrift Store Paintings. In the former, Shaw used standardized seventeen-by-fourteen-inch canvases or sheets of paper to chronicle the travails of a teenager named Billy who came of age in the 1970s. He took on the styles of psychedelic-poster artists, comic-book illustrators, various avant-garde artists (such as Frank Stella, Tom Wesselmann, and John Baldessari), pulp-fiction cover designers, and erotic draftsmen, among many others, in the telling of his protagonist's story. Shaw found another way to satiate his interests in the glut of global image production in Thrift Store Paintings, a collection of over four hundred amateur paintings the artist has amassed since 1974, first shown together in 1990 in an exhibition and publication. None of the works were actually painted by Shaw, but his selection of them, coupled

From Jim Shaw's My Mirage (1986–91) (left to right):
THE GOLDEN BOOK OF KNOWLEDGE, 1989, gouache on board, 17 x 14 inches
Collections of Eileen Harris Norton and Peter Norton, Santa Monica

CONCEPTUAL ART (JOHN BALDESSARI), 1987, oil on canvas, 17 x 14 inches
Private collection

EASTER ON MY BRAIN, 1990, acrylic on paper, 17 x 14 inches
The Museum of Contemporary Art, Los Angeles. Gift of Thea Westreich and Ethan Wagner

15

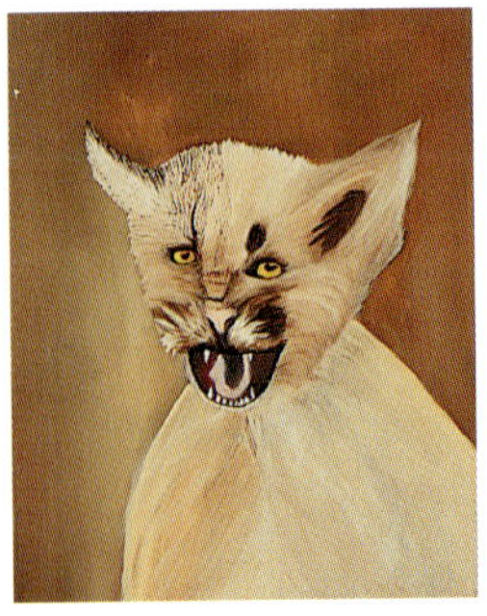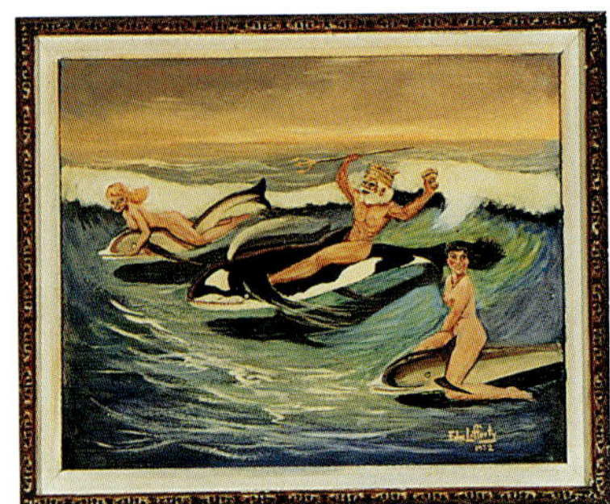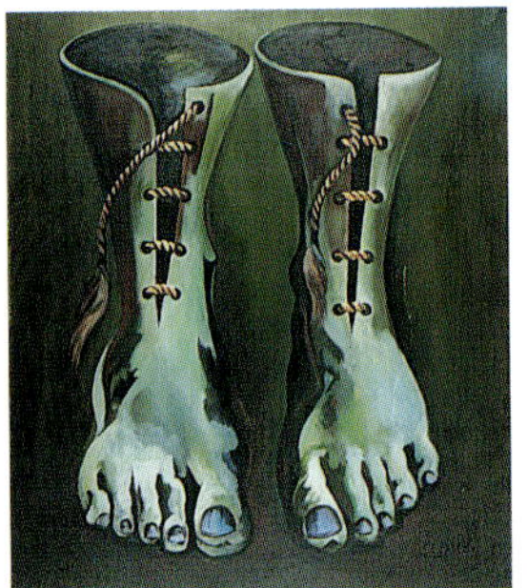

 with the dry descriptive titles he gave them, constitute a kind of
meta-painting project that is not so far removed from the practices of
Richter, Polke, and Kippenberger.

Like these predecessors, the seven artists included in "Painting in
Tongues"—Kai Althoff, Gillian Carnegie, Mark Grotjahn, Lucy McKenzie,
Rodney McMillian, Ivan Morley, and Anselm Reyle—keep their painting practices open and viable by embracing impulses and conditions that may make
their work appear outwardly inconsistent. It is often difficult to construct a simple narrative summarizing their concerns, style, or relation
to history, since their work bucks the instinct towards a single style
or voice. At the expense of their well-defined square in the grid of history, they have opted for a pulsating mutating blob of activity that is
sure to be more rewarding in the long run.

At a time when painting has achieved a decided renaissance—with considerable institutional, commercial, and critical attention bestowed upon
it—it seems worthwhile to closely examine the work of artists who are truly
pushing the tradition forward. Not content to narrowly follow a single
line of questioning, these artists have each found ways to work against
a single recognizable hand and, in so doing, have introduced a raft of
subjectivities into their palette of options. When looking closely at each
artist's extremely varied output, patterns and connections emerge that

From Jim Shaw's Thrift Store Paintings (left to right):
Artist unknown, PINK MOUNTAIN LION ON BROWN BACKGROUND, n.d., oil on board, 20 x 16 inches
Collection of Ellen Kaufman

Edwin Lafferty, NEPTUNE AND NYMPHS ASTRIDE SEA MAMMALS, n.d., acrylic on board,
27 1/2 x 34 1/2 inches
Collection of Michael Walker

L. Grace, FRANKENSTEIN-MAGRITTE BOOTS, n.d., oil on canvas, 30 x 26 inches
Collection of Jim Shaw

link their works together and give them order and meaning—although by choice they have deferred the gestalt of a single work to a broader view that takes their entire practice into account. This is not to say that they do not make stunning work when viewed individually, but it is in the aggregate that their work truly reverberates.

We are still only witnessing the early stages of the development of these young artists' careers, but the maturity and sustained activity each has shown thus far gives us a sense of the potential of their undertakings. Recognizing the seriousness of their quests, but not knowing exactly where they will lead, is an exciting position to be in as a viewer. For, as Ehrenzweig wrote, "If we could map out the entire way ahead, no further search would be needed. As it is, the creative thinker has to make a decision about his route without having the full information needed for his choice. This dilemma belongs to the essence of creativity."[13] We are privileged to bear witness to that essence.

NOTES:

1. Julia Kristeva, "Word, Dialogue and Novel" (1966), in The Kristeva Reader (New York: Columbia University Press, 1986), 48.

2. Felix Zdenek, ed., Francis Picabia: The Late Works, 1933-1953 (Ostfildern-Ruit, Germany: Hatje Cantz), 7.

3. Anton Ehrenzweig, The Hidden Order of Art: A Study in the Psychology of Artistic Imagination (Berkeley: University of California Press, 1967), xii.

4. Ibid., 67.

5. Ibid., 49.

6. Walter Benjamin, "One-Way Street" (1923-26), in Marcus Bullock and Michael W. Jennings, eds., Walter Benjamin: Selected Writings, Volume 1, 1913-1926 (Cambridge, Massachusetts: The Belknap Press of Harvard University Press, 1996), 446.

7. Gerhard Richter, quoted in Hans-Ulrich Obrist, ed., Gerhard Richter The Daily Practice of Painting: Writings and Interviews 1962-1993 (Cambridge, Massachusetts: The MIT Press, 1995), 58.

8. Anke Kempkes, "Dear Painter, Paint for Me" (1981), in Eva Meyer-Hermann and Susanne Neuberger, eds., Nach Kippenberger/After Kippenberger (Vienna: Schlebrügge, 2003), 37.

9. Lucy McKenzie, "Now That This Has Been Done It Will Never Have To Be Done Again," in Nach Kippenberger, 191.

10. Timothy Martin, "Virtual and Nonvirtual Facture: A Tale of Two Hands (Draft 1)," in A History of the Renaissance Society 1990-2001 (Chicago: The Renaissance Society, 2004), 119.

11. Ibid.

12. Ibid.

13. Ehrenzweig, The Hidden Order of Art, xii.

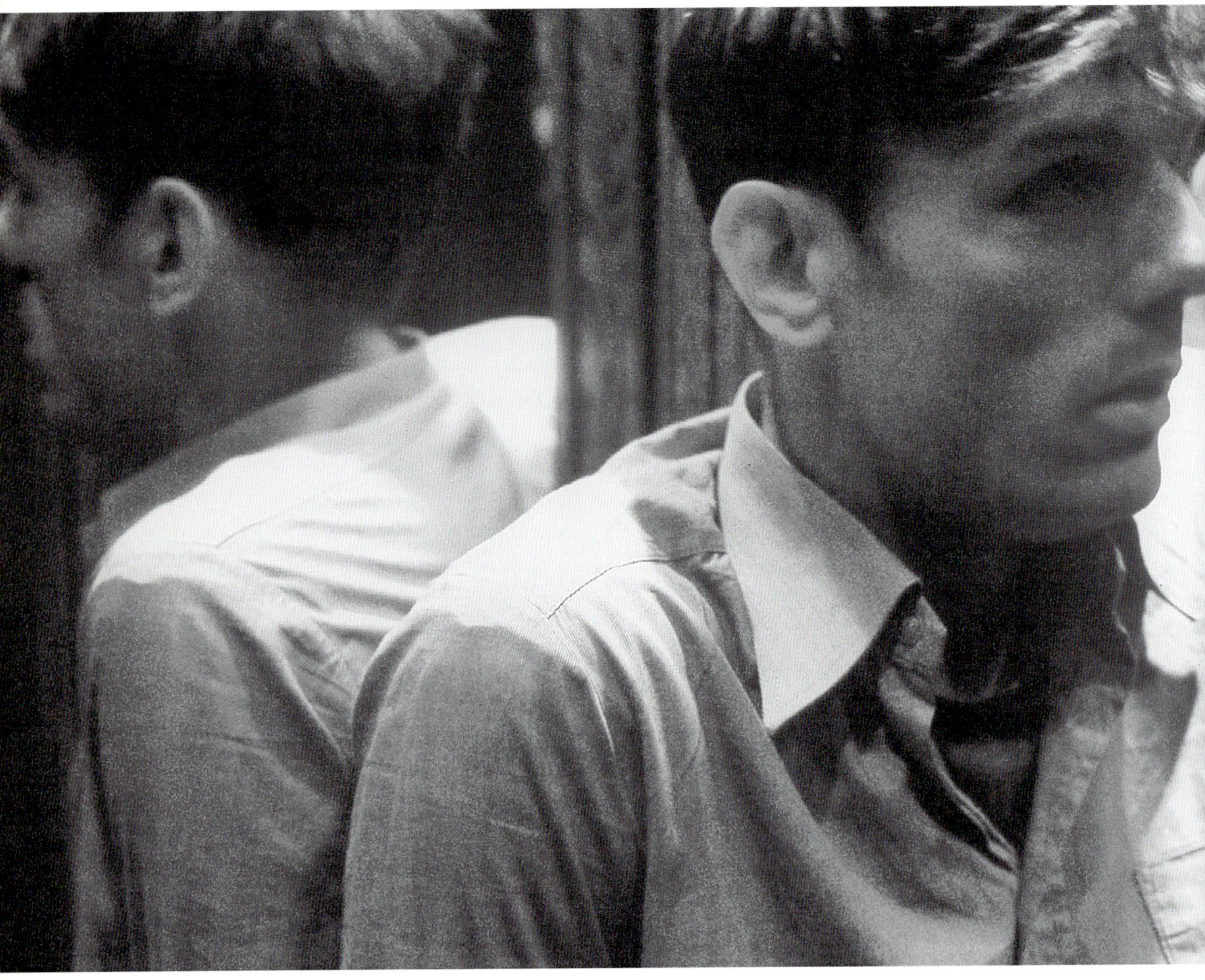

b. 1966, Cologne, Germany;
lives in Cologne

Selected Solo and Two-Person Exhibitions

2005 Acme, Los Angeles
2004 "Immo," Simultanhalle, Cologne, Germany
(exh. cat.)
"Kai Althoff: Kai Kein Respekt (Kai No
Respect)," The Institute of Contemporary
Art, Boston; and Museum of Contemporary
Art, Chicago (exh. cat.)
2003 "Kai Althoff & Abel Auer: 'Vom Monte
Scherbelino Sehen,'" Diözesanmuseum,
Freising, Germany (exh. cat.)
2002 "Kai Althoff und Armin Krämer," Kunst-
verein, Braunschweig, Germany (exh. cat.)
2001 "Impulse," Anton Kern Gallery, New York
"Aus Dir," Galerie Daniel Buchholz,
Cologne, Germany (exh. cat.)
2000 "Hau ab, Du Scheusal," Galerie Neu,
Berlin (exh. cat.)

"Stigmata aus Grossmannssucht,"
Galerie Ascan Crone, Hamburg, Germany
(exh. cat.)
1999 "Ein noch zu weiches Gewese der Urian
Bündner," Galerie Christian Nagel,
Cologne, Germany

Selected Group Exhibitions

2005 "The Triumph of Painting," The Saatchi
Gallery, London
2003 "Pittura," Museo Correr, Venice Biennale,
Venice, Italy
"deutschemalereizweitausenddrei,"
Kunstverein, Frankfurt, Germany
(exh. cat.)
2002 "Cher Peintre, Lieber Maler, Dear Painter:
Peintures figuratives depuis l'ultime

Kai Althoff

Painting in Tongues

Picabia," Centre Georges Pompidou, Paris;
Kunsthalle, Vienna; and Schirn Kunsthalle,
Frankfurt, Germany (exh. cat.)
"Drawing Now: Eight Propositions," The
Museum of Modern Art, New York (exh. cat.)
1999 "Ars Viva 98/99," Portikus, Frankfurt,
Germany; Brandenburgische Kunstsammlungen,
Cottbus, Germany; and Kunstverein,
Braunschweig, Germany (exh. cat.)

Selected Bibliography

- Cotter, Holland. "Hometown of Utopia and
Dissent." New York Times, 23 July 2004, E27, 29.
- Harris, Susan. "Kai Althoff at Anton Kern."
Art in America 90, no. 7 (July 2002): 100.
- Holert, Tom. "Band of Outsiders: The Art
of Kai Althoff." Artforum 40, no. 2
(October 2002): 124–29.
- Kai Althoff: Gebärde und Ausdruck. Berlin:
Lukas & Sternberg, 2002. Essays by Michaela
Eichwald, Anke Kempkes, Bernd Koehler, and
Jutta Koether.
- Kimmelman, Michael. "Kai Althoff at Anton
Kern Gallery." New York Times, 23 November
2001, E36.
- Rimanelli, David. "Kai Althoff at the
Institute of Contemporary Art, Boston."
Artforum 43, no. 1 (September 2004): 260–61.
- Rosenberg, Angela. "Kai Althoff: General
Rehearsals for a New Language." Flash Art 34,
no. 224 (May–June 2002): 94–97. Interview
with the artist.
- Saltz, Jerry. "History Painting: Kai
Althoff and the Return of the Repressed."
Village Voice (4 December 2001): 69.
Review of Anton Kern Gallery exhibition.

Kai Althoff's artistic output includes music, video, installations, sculptures, and paintings that are intensely personal, even private. In many ways, Althoff's work is autobiographical, but attempting to uncover specific biographical references is neither particularly fruitful, nor recommended by the artist.[1] What is more rewarding is to appreciate how the artist uses episodes from his own history to open a window to the changing social, political, and cultural landscape of post-1960s Germany. By variously tracing, memorializing, and conjecturing events as he might have witnessed them, he provides a more general evocation of the period. Sampling a range of cultural and political phenomena, he adapts his style and method of presentation to "fit" his subjects.

For instance, in Erwachsen werden, Fabio (1992), which suggests the travails of an adolescent boy coming to terms with his gay sexuality, he used loosely applied watercolors and an illustrator's shorthand to evoke a mixture of children's books and late-1970s Italian chic. Hakelhug (1996)—a project comprising objects, drawings, and paintings that documents an ex–Kraut-rock bass player who retreats to the countryside to form a commune —partakes of a much darker sensibility, involving brooding portraits of the long-haired, mustachioed protagonist as well as earthy clay figurines. Through this project, the artist expanded his own artistic repertoire by taking on the persona of an invented character, a strategy that enabled him "to make work as if he is Hakelhug."[2]

The variety found in Althoff's work is due in part to his performative practice of taking on alternative identities, as well as his interest in and cultivation of collaborative projects such as his band Workshop. In the latter, authorship is obfuscated, with imaginary contributors listed on albums or quoted on record sleeves.[3] Occasionally, such heterogeneity plays out within a single installation: for his 2001 exhibition "Impulse" at Anton Kern Gallery, New York, a wide range of artistic modes was deployed, from process-oriented abstractions to expressionistic figuration, faux-naïve architectural renderings, appropriated photography, and religious vignettes. A sense of continuous time also disappeared in this mix, with imagery referencing everything from 1970s café culture, early twentieth-century dress codes, and early Christian iconography. Some works, such as Untitled (Two Men and

---

1. Kai Althoff, in conversation with the author, 21 October 2004.

2. Nicholas Baume, "Feel It All," in Kai Kein Respekt (Kai No Respect), exh. cat. (Boston: The Institute of Contemporary Art; and Miami Beach: Bridge House Publishing, 2004), 21.

3. Ibid., 11.

Woman with Bicycle) (2001), evoke this time warp in a single canvas; one is made aware of the broad sweep of time and subject matter that Althoff seeks to activate in his work, a kaleidoscopic index of the forces that have conspired to shape his sense of reality.

In his 2004 installation for Simultanhalle, an alternative gallery located in the suburbs of Cologne, Germany, the artist used a different device to break up the single authorial mode and embrace a spectrum of temporal associations. The exhibition, titled "Immo," might have appeared at first glance to be a flea market or rummage sale, with items propped up against walls or sitting on fabric tarps spread out on the ground. The range of objects displayed—including grandfather clocks, bric-a-brac, photographs, mannequins, old televisions, a Victorian baby carriage, mirrors, wrapping paper, and a large selection of paintings and drawings—also strengthened this feeling. The artworks were displayed casually among the "clutter," avoiding any hierarchy among objects and allowing the associative qualities of the mundane materials to create a context. It would not be hard to imagine these materials as the result of decades of accumulation. Brooding Symbolist paintings done in a style that might have been popular in the early 1960s, Pop-Victorian images redolent of late-60s visual culture, freewheeling 70s skateboarding imagery, and anarchic early-80s abstractions countered with suave images from Italian men's fashion magazines of the same time all compete for attention. A lingering sense of love, loneliness, and even death pervaded the silent and unpeopled scenario to transcend the personal and speak of a universal early midlife reckoning. "Immo" took stock of a life lived, sketching out the passage of time through paintings, sculptures, photographs, and drawings of varying sizes, styles, and methods. Taken on their own, they were gripping, but when considered as distinct yet interrelated parts of an ever-expanding mosaic, they became engrossing.

WORKS IN THE EXHIBITION

UNTITLED, 1981
Mixed media
Approximately 19 3/4 x 27 1/2 inches
Collection of the artist, Cologne

BIG BEN, 2004
Collage, sprayed color, oil, plastic foil,
and fabric on fabric
34 1/2 x 32 1/4 inches
Collection of Craig Robins, Miami

UNTITLED, 2004
Oil sprayed on fabric
24 x 25 1/4 inches
Collection of the artist, Cologne

UNTITLED, 2004
Collage and fringed border on paper
19 3/4 x 27 1/2 inches
Collection of the artist, Cologne

UNTITLED, 2004
Oil-sprayed fabric
27 3/4 x 25 inches
Collection of the artist, Cologne

UNTITLED, 2004
Oil-sprayed fabric on fabric
19 x 22 1/4 inches
Collection of Martin and Rebecca Eisenberg,
New York

UNTITLED, 2004
Collage, lacquer, and oil on fabric
24 x 22 1/2 inches
Collection of Gerald Fineberg, Wellesley,
Massachusetts

UNTITLED, 2004
Oil on canvas
32 1/2 x 27 1/2 inches
Private collection, New York

UNTITLED, 2004
Oil, sprayed color, lacquer, and dispersion
on fabric
39 3/4 x 39 inches
Collection of Gustavo Hernandez, Miami

UNTITLED, 2004
Sprayed color, latex, and oil on fabric
27 x 20 1/4 inches
Collection of Matthew Kozol, Boston

UNTITLED, 2004
Photograph and sprayed color on fabric
15 x 30 inches
Collection of Rena Conti and Ivan Moskowitz,
Brookline, Massachusetts

UNTITLED, 2004
Printing screen, spray paint, ink, and pen
on paper
14 x 16 1/2 inches
The Museum of Modern Art, New York

UNTITLED, 2004
Pen and ink on paper
Five works: 11 1/4 x 12; 11 x 12 1/2;
11 x 12 3/4; 13 1/2 x 11; and 11 x 14 inches
The Museum of Modern Art, New York

UNTITLED, 2004
Sprayed color, leather on wrapping paper,
and antique frame
35 x 27 inches
Ovitz Family Collection, Los Angeles

UNTITLED, 2004
Lambswool on cotton
35 x 30 5/16 inches
Private collection, Berlin

UNTITLED, 2004
Plastic foil, ink, pen, and sprayed color
on wrapping paper
19 x 13 inches
Private collection, Munich

UNTITLED, 2004
Paper, marine varnish, and oil on fabric
21 1/2 x 21 1/2 inches
Collection of Sam and Shanit Schwartz,
Los Angeles

UNTITLED, 2004
Sprayed color on silk
34 1/4 x 36 1/4 inches
Collection of Beth Swofford, Los Angeles

UNTITLED, 2004
Oil and lacquer on fabric
27 1/2 x 29 1/2 inches
Collection of Joel Wachs

UNTITLED, 2004
Ink, collage, pen, and spray paint on paper
9 x 11 1/2 inches
Collection of Dianne Wallace, New York

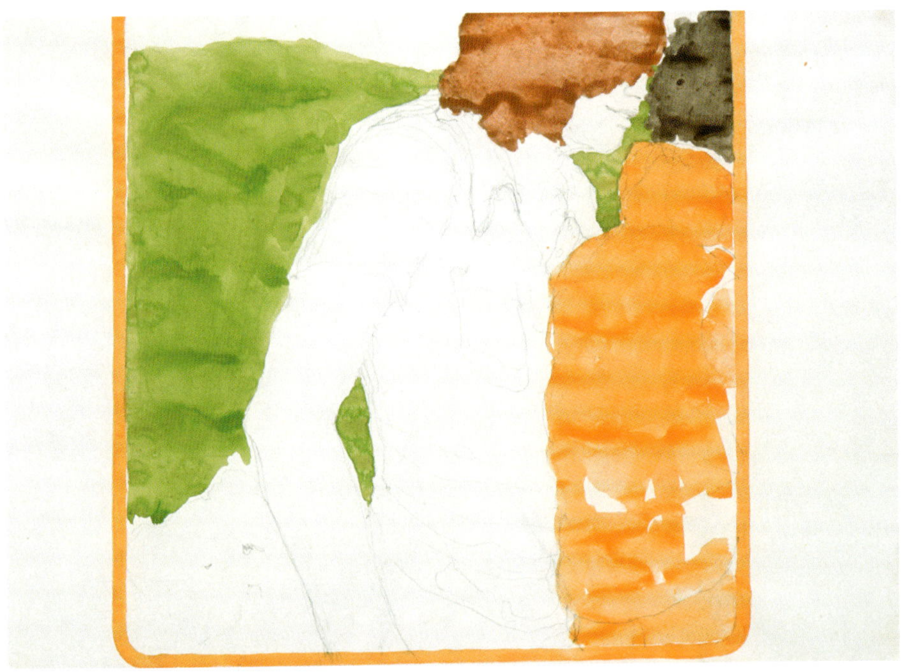

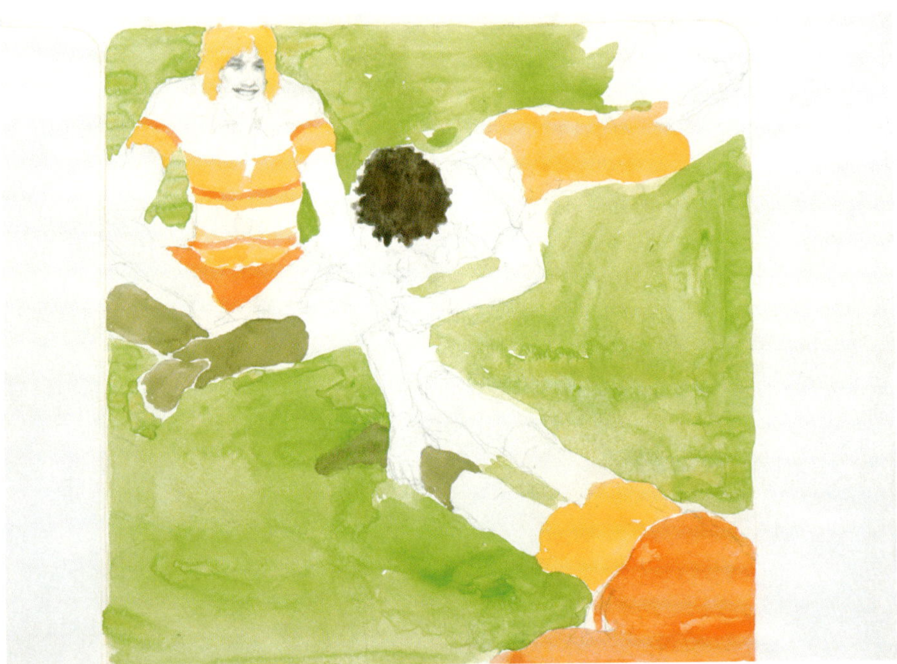

Details of ERWACHSEN WERDEN, FABIO (Growing up, Fabio), 1992
Acrylic, crayon, and pencil on paper
Sixteen paintings: 11 7/16 x 16 9/16 inches each
Collection of Gregorio Magnani, London

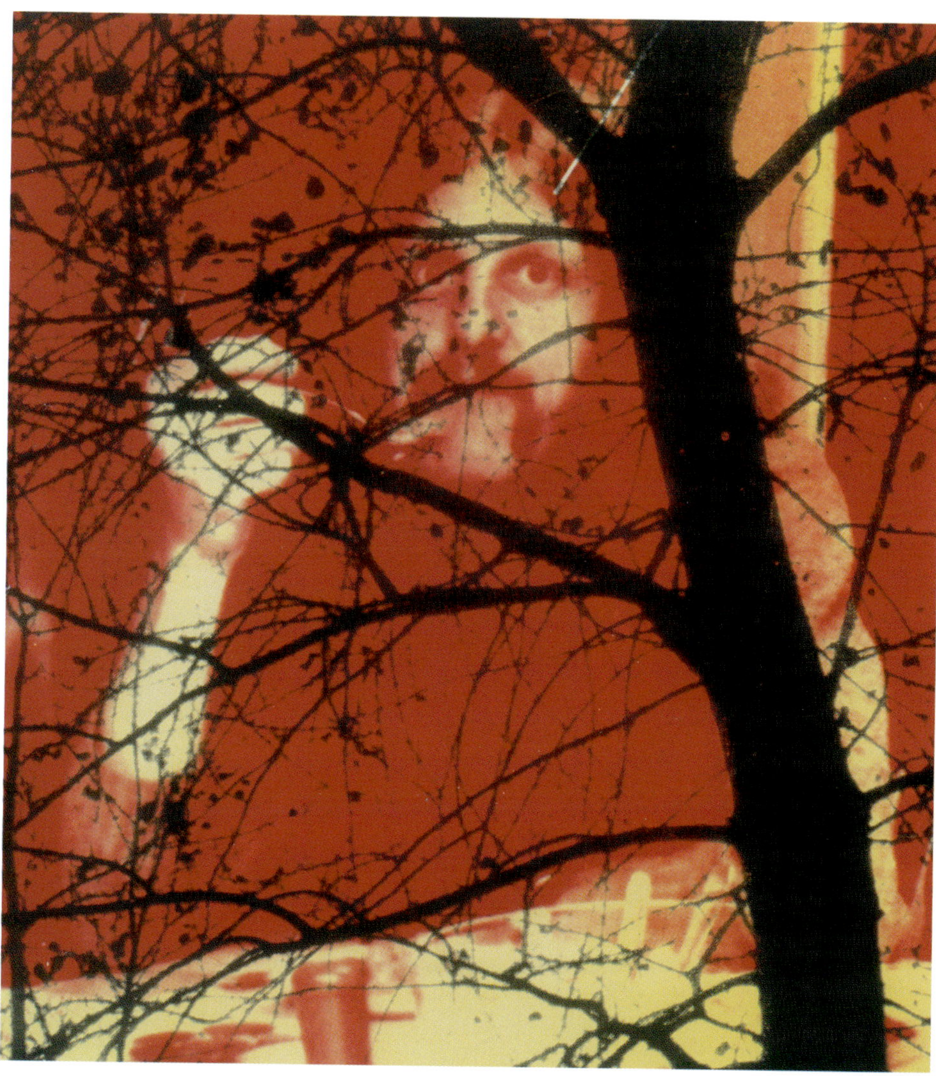

UNTITLED, from HAKELHUG (1996)
Color photocopy on paper
12 3/16 x 11 1/4 inches
Collection of Alexander Schröder, Berlin

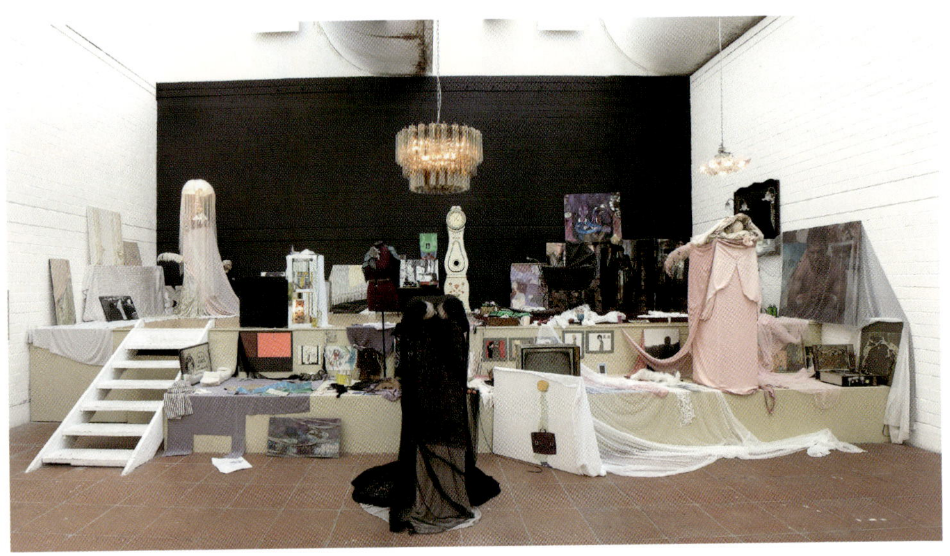

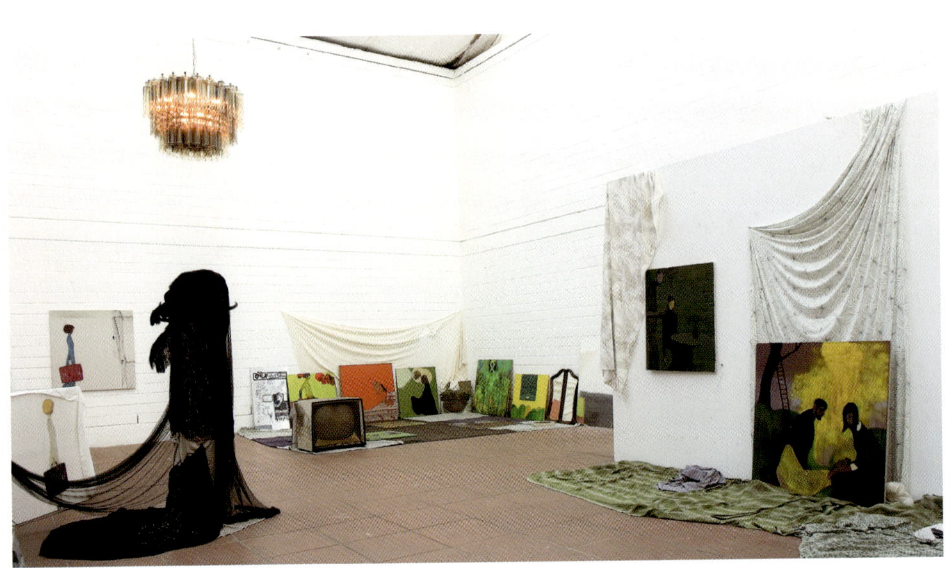

"Immo," installation at Simultanhalle, Cologne, Germany, 2004

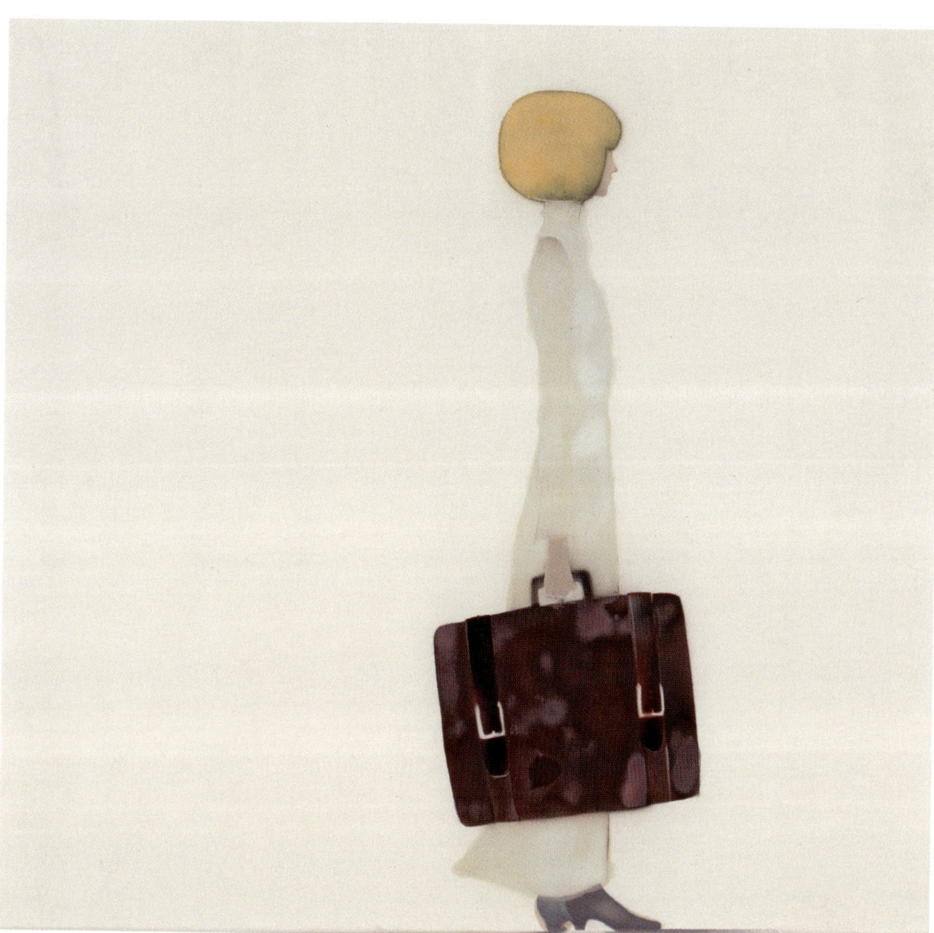

UNTITLED, 2004
Sprayed color on silk
34 1/4 x 36 1/4 inches
Collection of Beth Swofford, Los Angeles

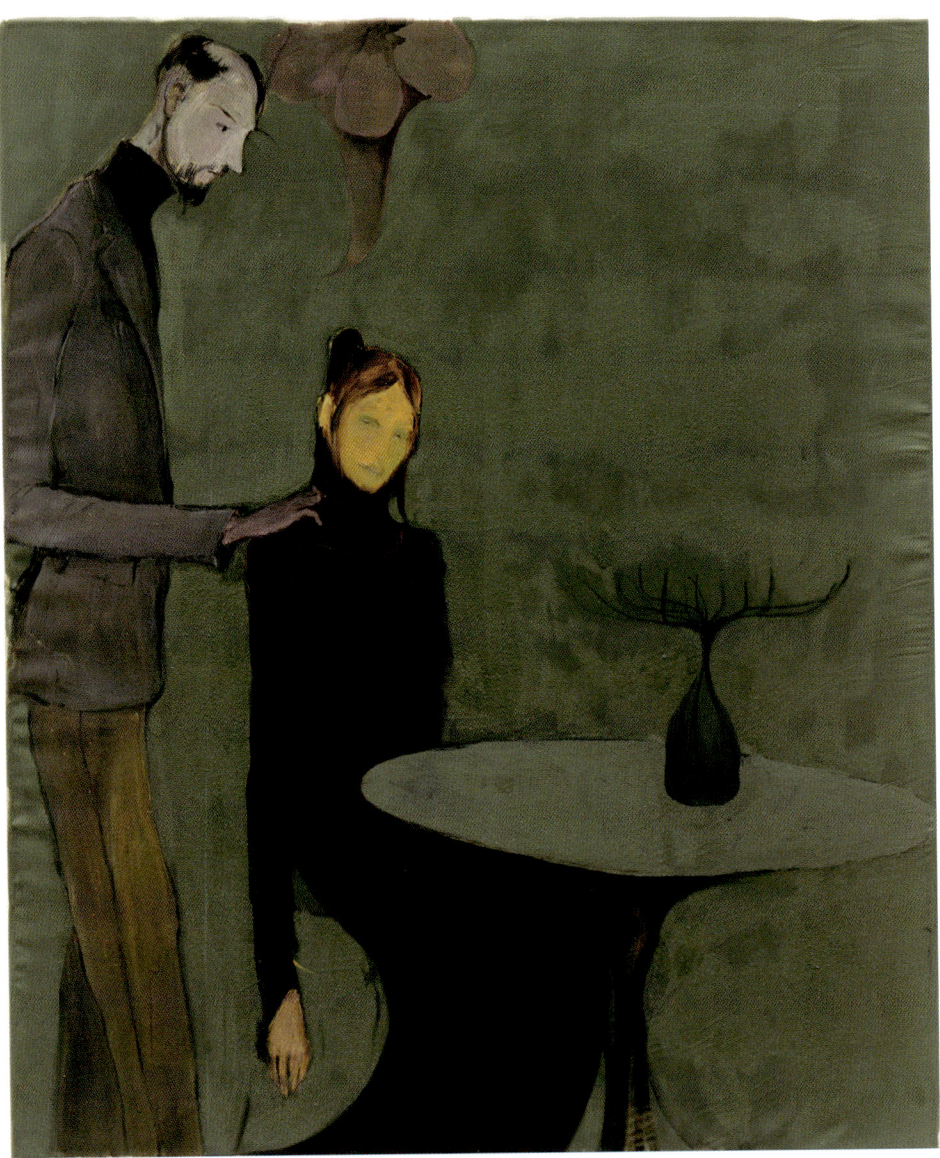

28

UNTITLED, 2004
Oil and lacquer on fabric
32 1/2 x 27 3/8 inches
Private collection, New York

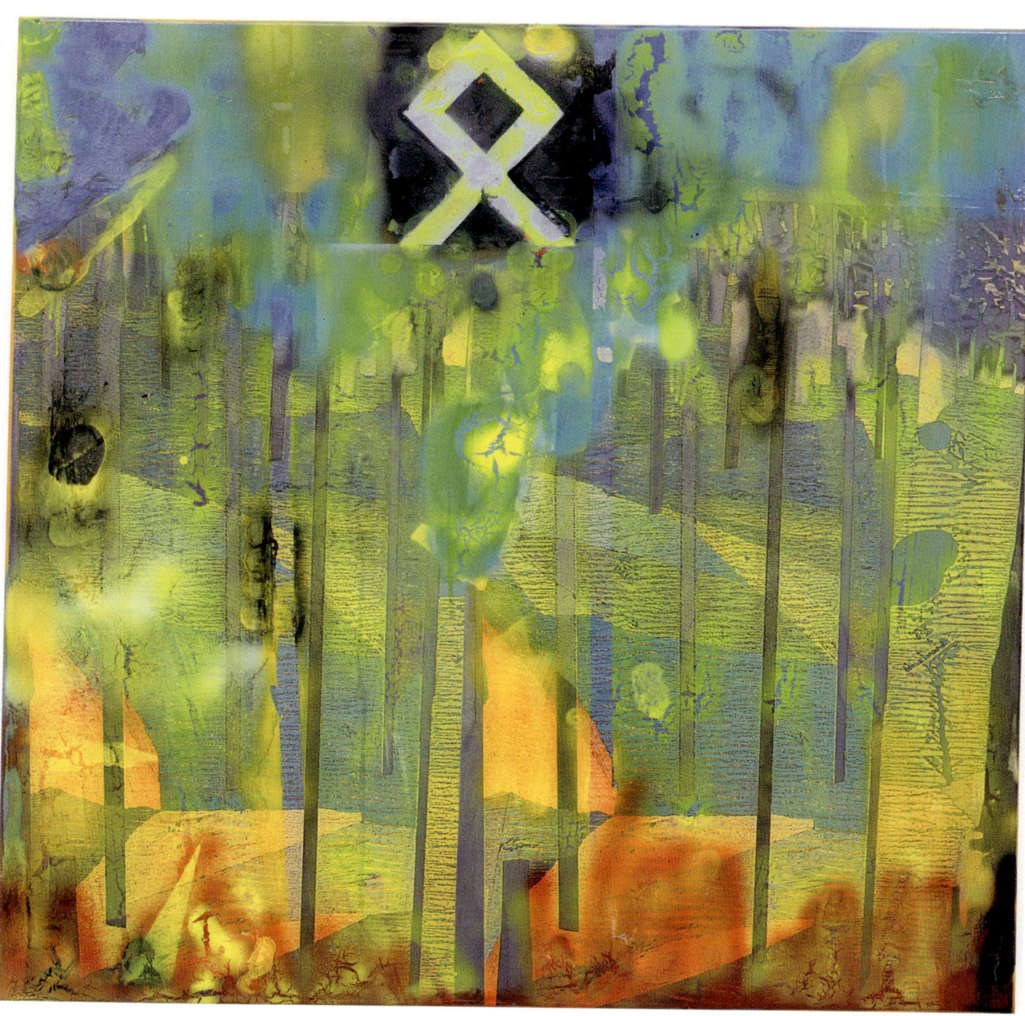

UNTITLED, 2004
Dispersion, spray, and wrapping paper on fabric
33 1/4 x 35 7/16 inches
Collection of Toni and Daniel Holtz

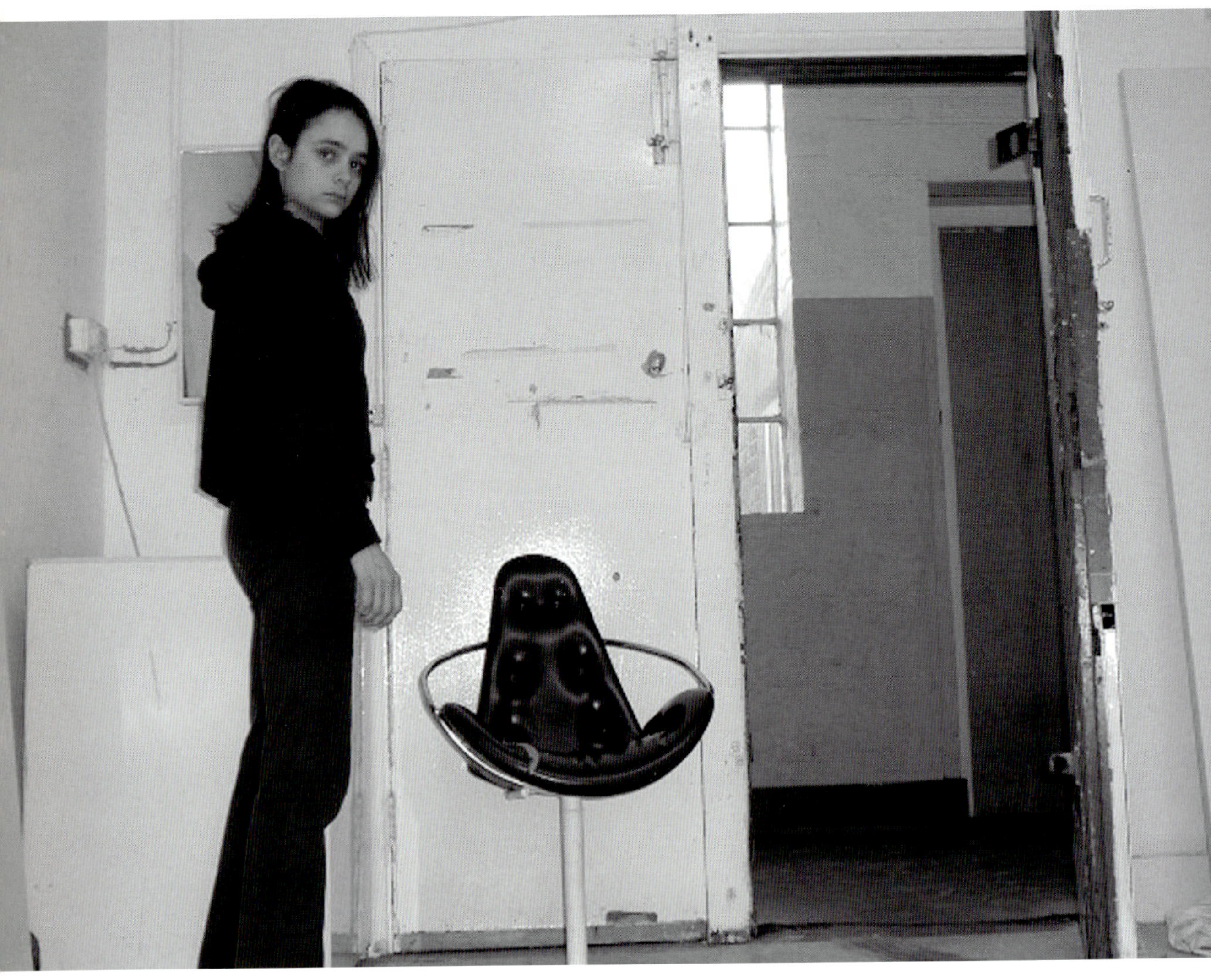

b. 1971, Suffolk, England;
lives in London

Selected Solo Exhibitions

2005 Cabinet, London
2004 Galerie Gisela Capitain, Cologne,
     Germany
2003 Andrea Rosen Gallery, New York
2002 Cabinet, London
2000 Andrea Rosen Gallery, New York
1999 Cabinet, London

Selected Group Exhibitions

2005 Turner Prize 2005 Exhibition, Tate
     Britain, London
2002 "The House of Fiction," Sammlung Hauser
     & Wirth, Lokremise, St. Gallen,
     Switzerland
2001 "Hotel Sub Rosa," Cabinet, London;
     and Marc Foxx, Los Angeles
     "Extended Painting," Monica De Cardenas,
     Milan, Italy
2000 "Malerei 6," Monika Sprüth, Cologne,
     Germany
1998 "New Contemporaries 98," Camden Arts
     Centre, London; and The Tea Factory,
     Liverpool, England (exh. cat.)

Gillian Carnegie

Painting in Tongues

Selected Bibliography

- Becker, Ilka. "Alle unter einem Dach."
Texte zur Kunst 10, no. 40 (December 2000):
147–50.
- Burrows, David. "New Contemporaries 98 at
Camden Arts Centre." *Art Monthly*, no. 219
(September 1998): 219–20.
- Johnson, Ken. "Gillian Carnegie at Andrea
Rosen." *New York Times*, 12 May 2000, E38.
- Panting, Lisa. "Gillian Carnegie: Bum
Paintings." *Art Monthly*, no. 250 (October
2001): 20–21.
- Staple, Polly. "The Finishing Touch."
Frieze, no. 64 (January–February 2002): 72–75.

It is easy to become enthralled by the potent energy and beauty of Gillian Carnegie's paintings, but one can best appreciate the ambition of her undertaking when multiple works are seen side by side. Her subject matter, viewpoint, palette, scale, and handling of paint change dramatically from work to work, building up a catalogue of imagery that is anything but singular. Though many of the subjects recur, the way they are painted rarely does, as one of Carnegie's primary motivations is to keep pushing her craft, often into areas where she feels less than comfortable or secure.[1]

These technical challenges imbue her paintings with a sense of risk, which is especially noticeable when she works within discredited or stale genres. Dusky still lifes such as Waltz I (2004), for example, could almost be seen as objects rescued from a secondhand shop. Featuring a vase of dried flowers against neutral drapery, Waltz I seems to have been soaking up secondhand smoke in a spinster's sitting room for decades. Waltz II (2004) offers the same palette and subject as Waltz I but from a different viewpoint, as if from another of the artist's memories. Beyond their superficial stodginess, Carnegie's still lifes possess painterly energy and compositional vigor, breathing new life into dead forms.

Carnegie's shifting style could be explained as an excavation of memory using various methods to picture a range of times and places, suggesting the instability of perception. Voi (2004) shows a faded vista down a verdant path, painted in a clumpy scumbled style that went out of fashion in the late 1960s, perhaps tying the image to a deeper stratum of the memory bank. Greener (2004) adopts the same vantage point but features richer, more saturated hues and a less decrepit handling of paint, as if to communicate a more easily accessible recollection. Together, the works address the shifting ground of perception, subjectivity, and reflection, a central concern in her practice. The dream quality in Carnegie's work varies, sometimes communicating seemingly innocuous childhood memories as in May Queen Detail (2003), a small work on canvas later revisited in a larger

[1.] Gillian Carnegie, in conversation with the author, 16 October 2004.

painting on paper titled May Queen (2004). In these two works—as well as a 2003 charcoal drawing of the same title—the artist's technique of zooming in and out on the central female figure features different emphases and degrees of pictorial clarity that approximates the mutating significances of recurring dreams.

Absurdity and the nonsequitur also creep into her work from time to time. Pinata (2004), in which a bizarre rabbit figure is suspended from a stark armature within a vaguely tropical setting, breaks from Carnegie's human and nature scenes while mirroring the unpredictability of dream states and resisting an easy categorization of her overall output. Her visions can be ominous as well. For example, works in the ongoing Black Square series—which reveal considerable variety despite sharing the same title and dominant color—are characterized by an undercurrent of dread that complicates and enriches Carnegie's other paintings. Through powerful and evocative brushwork, the artist conjures trees, bramble, and earth amidst dark dank forests in these muscular and meaty paintings.

Another staple in the artist's repertoire of images is her own ass, which she renders from a number of angles, under different lighting conditions, and with a plurality of painterly touches. One constant is the cropping of the torso below the waist and above mid-thigh so that the frame is filled by her chosen subject with no possible distractions. In Brunette (2004), her cheeks are rendered with warm dappled brushstrokes as if they were Paul Cézanne's apples ripening in the sun; in Nude on White Linen (2002), pale creamy expanses of skin remind one of Edouard Manet's figures; and in Red (2004), lurid slapdash smears more akin to Marlene Dumas's work hint at the pornographic. Doubtless the gesture of putting her bum in the face of viewers is meant to be provocative in both an erotic and anti-bourgeois way, but it also functions as a feminist reclaiming of the contentious "gaze."

If one thinks of Carnegie's work as an ongoing investigation of the fragmentary and fleeting nature of memory, however, these self-portraits also serve as markers of the "now," capturing a state of being before it is dragged away into the past.

Focusing on a cherished aspect of her youthful beauty, they memorialize her body,
forestalling the inevitable forces of aging and gravity as only art can. A cynic
might be quick to trivialize these pieces as strategic grabs at shock or notoriety,
but when they are considered within the entirety of her practice they are shown to
be equals in a complicated network of attempts to give visual form to the vagaries
of time and memory.

WORKS IN THE EXHIBITION

BLUE CHEER, 2000
Oil on canvas
67 x 84 inches
Collection of Dean Valentine and
Amy Adelson, Los Angeles

CHAMELEON, 2002
Oil on canvas
54 x 68 inches
Collection of Dean Valentine and
Amy Adelson, Los Angeles

NO DEPRESSION, 2002
Oil on paper
20 x 14 inches
Private collection, Chicago

BLACK SQUARE, 2003
Oil on canvas
75 x 75 inches
Cranford Collection, London

BLACK SQUARE, 2003
Oil on paper
49 1/4 x 56 inches
Private collection, Germany

KALVIN, 2004
Oil on paper
22 x 15 1/2 inches
Collection of the artist, London

SECTION, 2004
Oil on canvas
20 x 18 inches
Collection of Mario Testino, London

MAISON MERLIN, 2005
Charcoal on paper
28 1/4 x 37 3/4 inches
Private collection
Courtesy of Cabinet, London

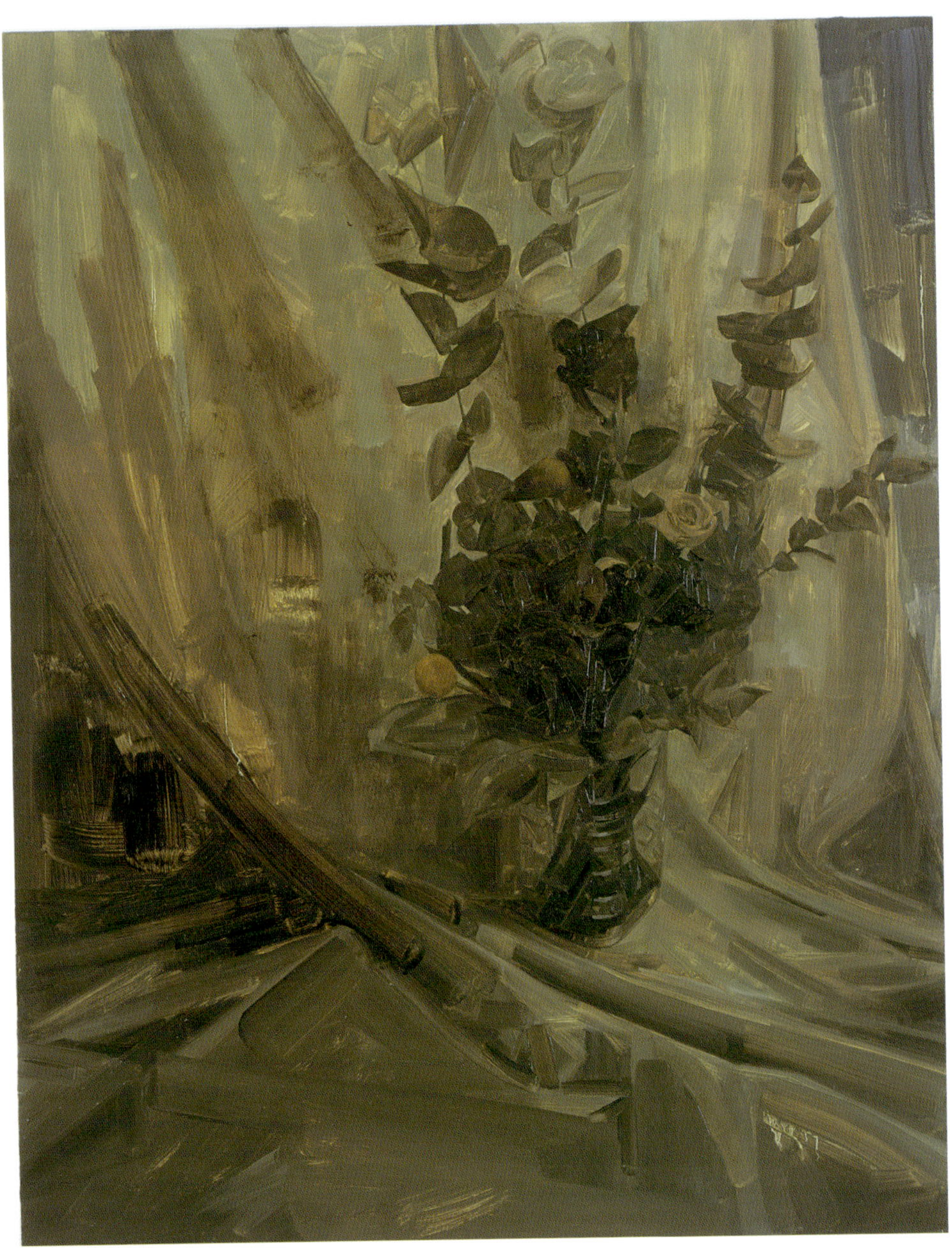

36

WALTZ I, 2004
Oil on board
29 x 23 inches
Private collection

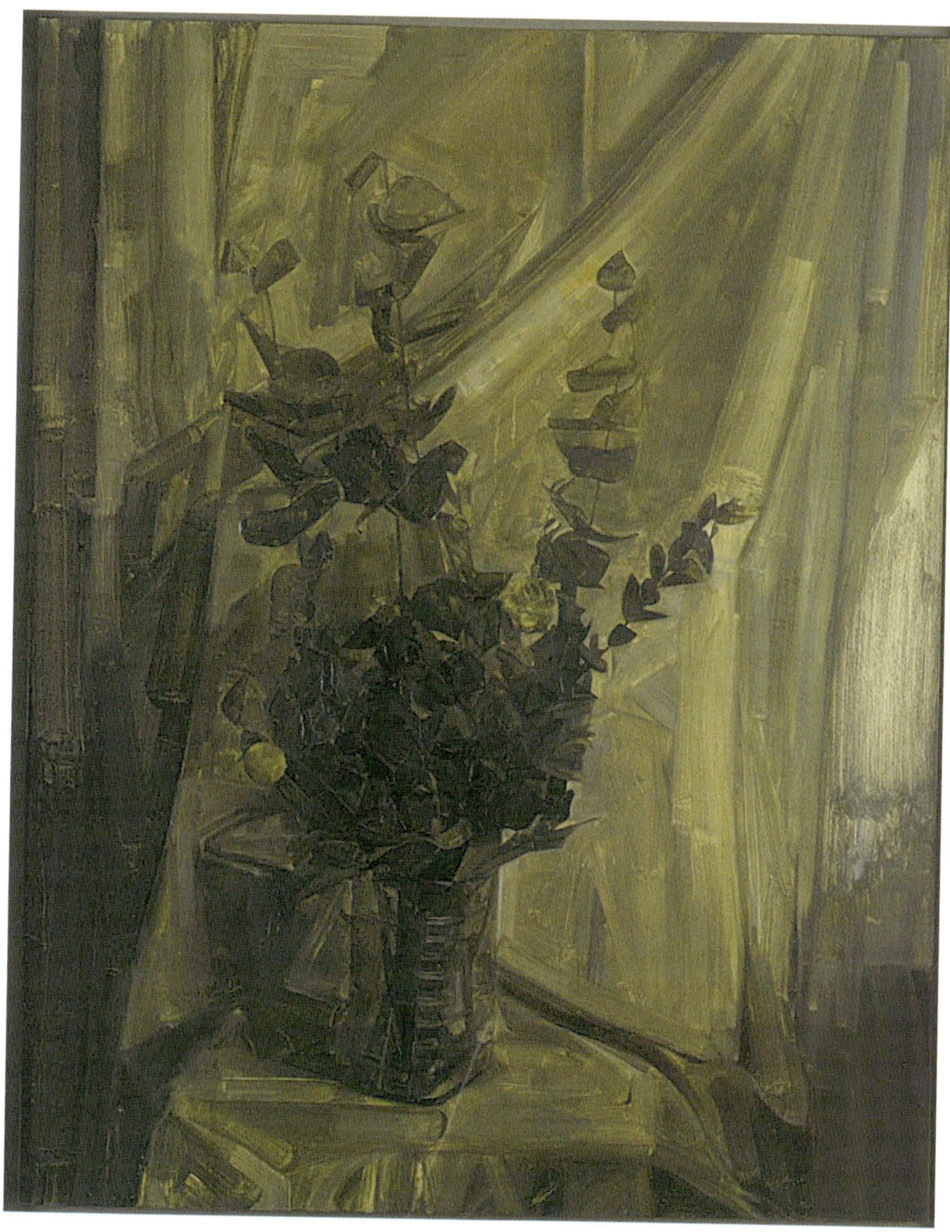

WALTZ II, 2004
Oil on paper
29 x 23 inches
Private collection

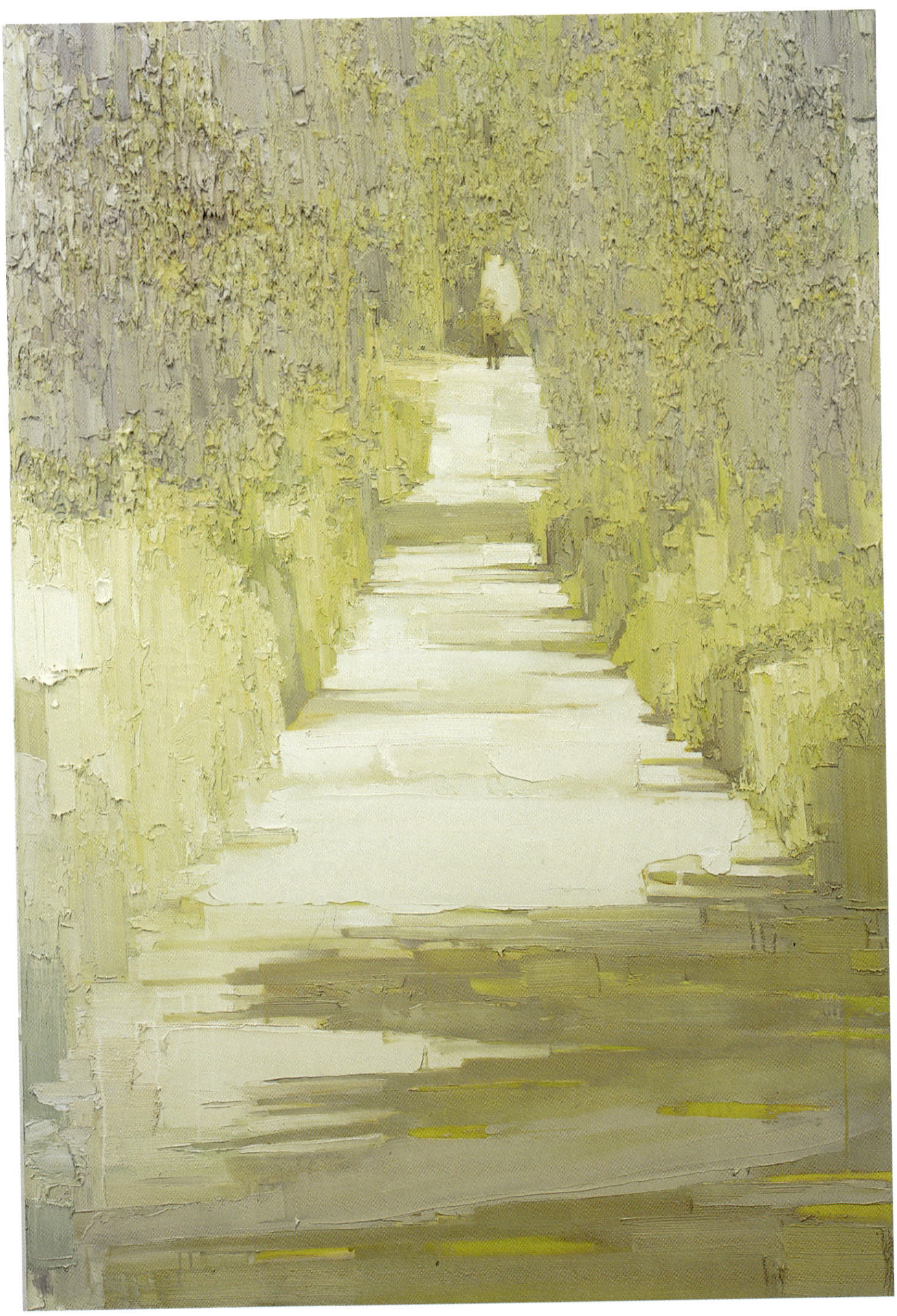

VOI, 2004
Oil on canvas
76 x 53 1/4 inches
Andrea Rosen Collection, New York

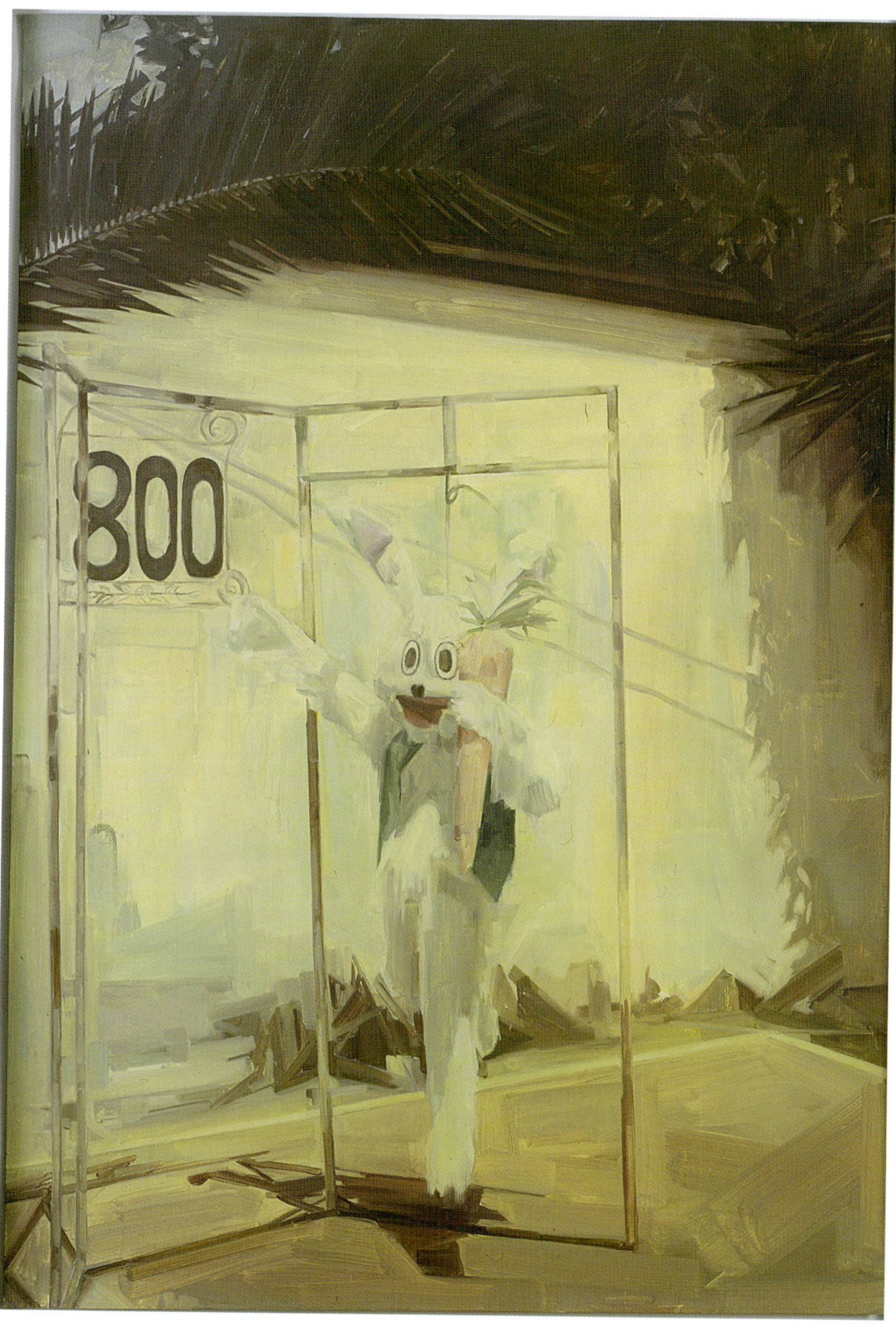

PINATA, 2004
Oil on paper
39 x 27 inches
Private collection

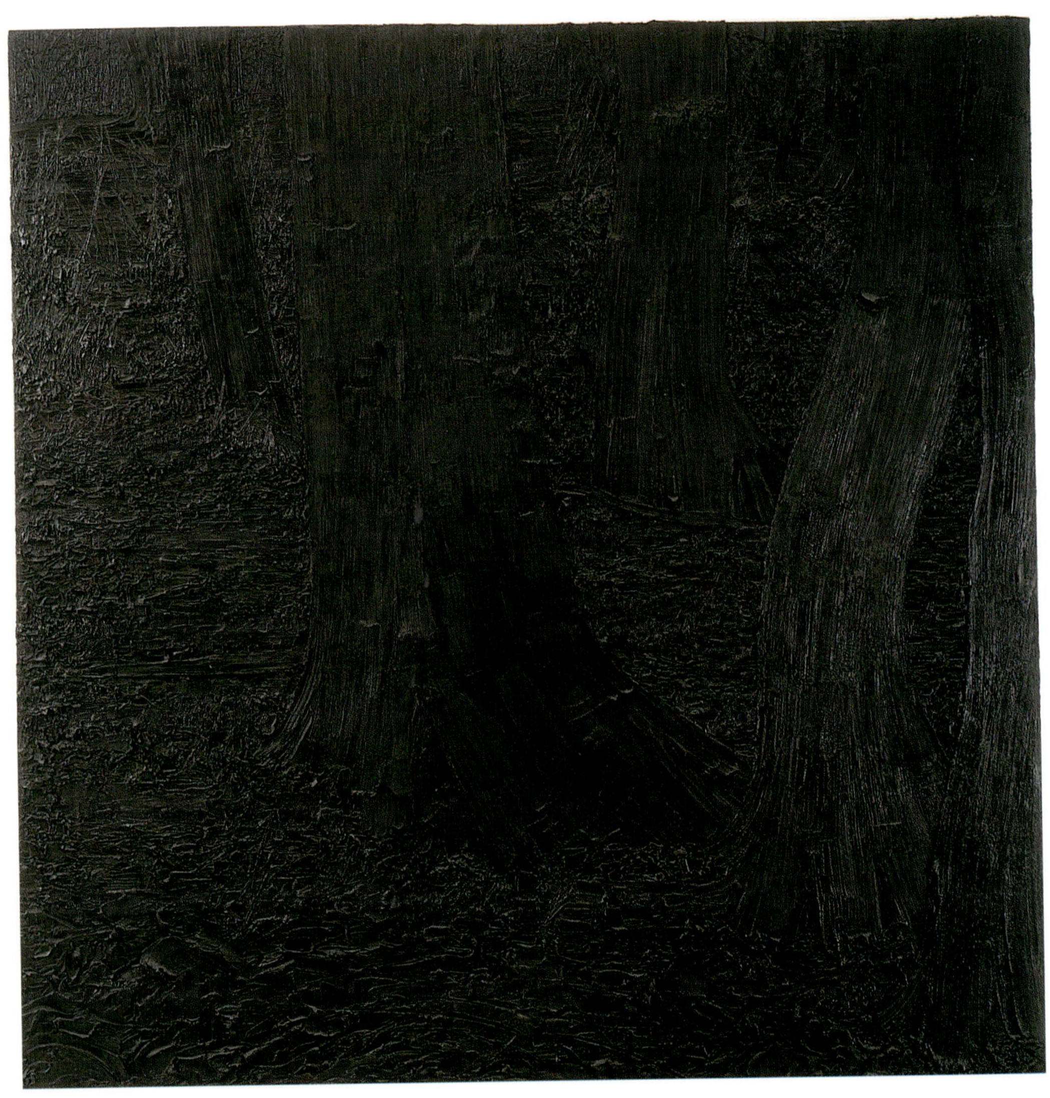

BLACK SQUARE, 2003
Oil on canvas
75 x 75 inches
Cranford Collection, London

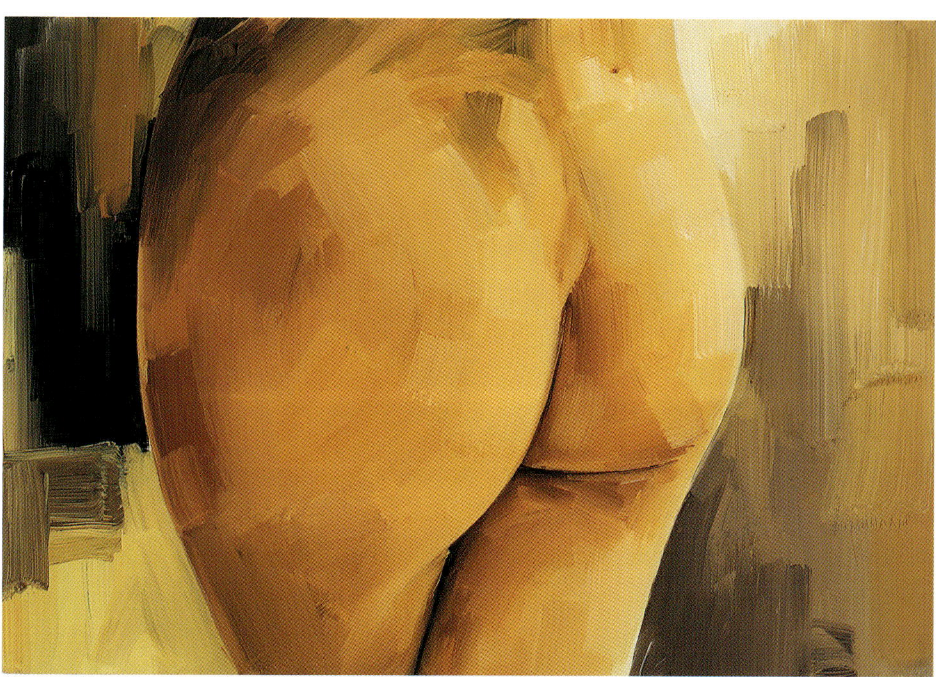

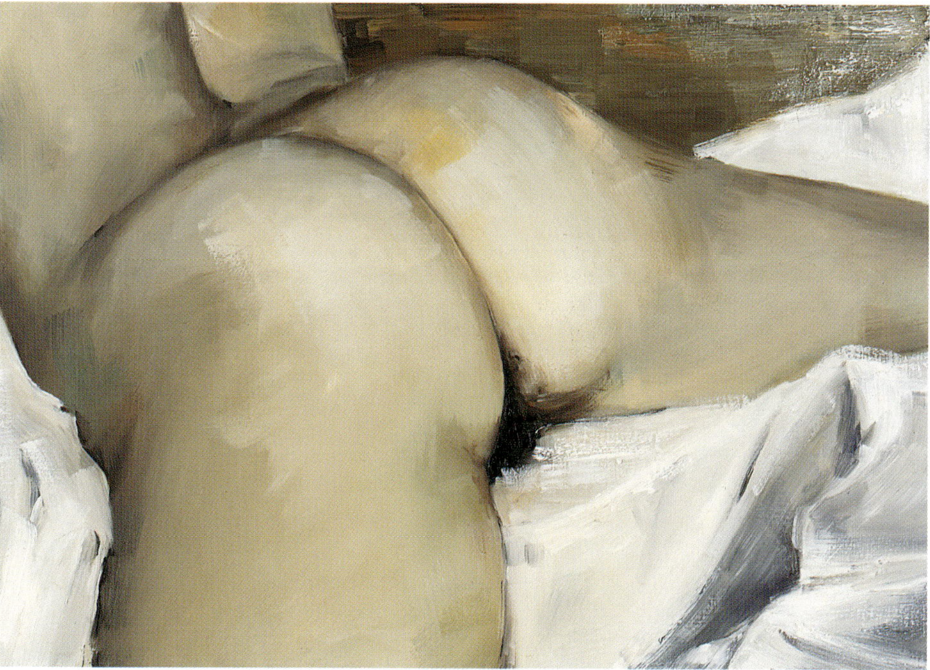

Top:
BRUNETTE, 2004
Oil on board
9 x 13 inches
Collection of Matt Aberle, Los Angeles

Bottom:
NUDE ON WHITE LINEN, 2002
Oil on board
9 x 13 inches
Private collection

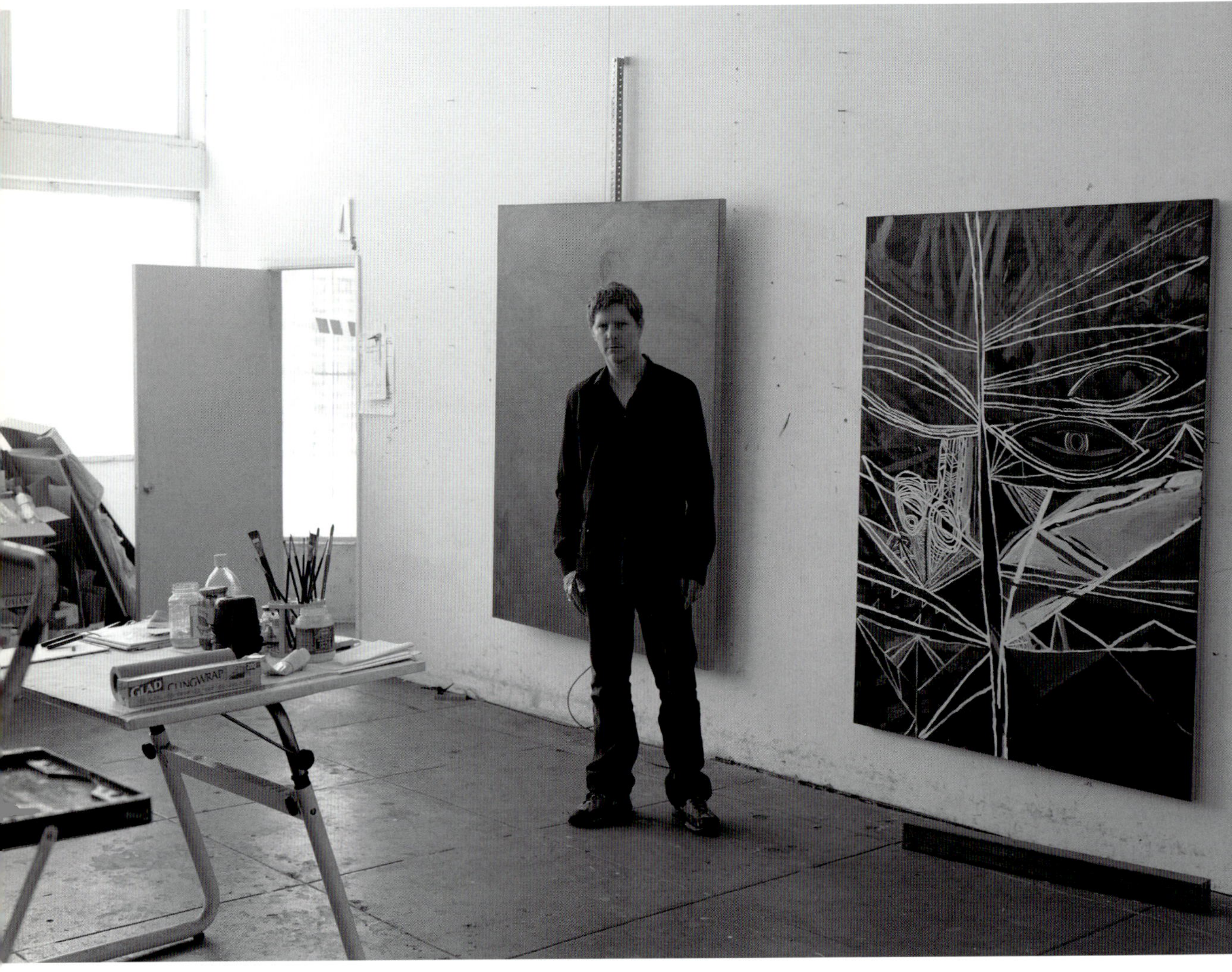

b. 1968, Pasadena, California;
lives in Los Angeles

Selected Solo Exhibitions

2005 Blum & Poe, Los Angeles
Stephen Friedman, London
"Mark Grotjahn: Drawings," Hammer
Museum, Los Angeles
2003 Anton Kern Gallery, New York
2002 "Mark Grotjahn: El gran burrito,"
Boom, Chicago
Blum & Poe, Santa Monica, California
2000 Blum & Poe, Santa Monica, California
1998 Blum & Poe, Santa Monica, California
"Flowers in the Office," Brent Petersen
Gallery, Los Angeles

Selected Group Exhibitions

2004 54th Carnegie International, Carnegie
Museum of Art, Pittsburgh (exh. cat.)

2002 "Play It as It Lays," London Institute
Gallery, London
2001 "Sharing Sunsets," Museum of Contemporary
Art, Tucson, Arizona
"Out of Bounds: Working Off Paper,"
Luckman Gallery, California State
University, Los Angeles
"Superman in Bed: Kunst der Gegenwart
und Fotografie Sammlung Schürmann,"
Museum am Ostwall, Dortmund, Germany
"David Brody, Mark Grotjahn, Wade Guyton,
Siobhan Liddell," Gorney Bravin + Lee,
New York
2000 "'00," Barbara Gladstone Gallery,
New York
"Drawings from Los Angeles," Studio
Guenzani, Milan, Italy
1999 "After the Gold Rush," Thread Waxing
Space, New York
1998 "Entropy at Home," Suermondt Ludwig
Museum, Aachen, Germany

Mark Grotjahn

Selected Bibliography

- Burton, Johanna. "Mark Grotjahn at
Anton Kern." Artforum 42, no. 4
(December 2003): 146–47.
- Helfand, Glen. "Mark Grotjahn, Brent
Petersen, Paul Sietsema." Bay Area Guardian
(San Francisco), 13 August 1997.
- Miles, Christopher. "Working Variables,
Switching Games: Mark Grotjahn." Artext,
no. 78 (fall 2002): 44–51.
- Pagel, David. "Trying to Fit In."
Los Angeles Times, 20 November 1998, F32.
Review of Blum & Poe exhibition.
- Smith, Roberta. "Mark Grotjahn at Anton
Kern Gallery." New York Times, 24 October
2003, E35.
- Trainor, James. "Rates of Exchange."
Frieze, no. 78 (October 2003): 116–17.

Over the past few years, Mark Grotjahn has created a series of Butterfly Paintings, geometric abstractions that tend to be built up of triangular patches of paint pivoting from
central Barnett Newmanesque stripes. Concurrently, Grotjahn has produced several other
bodies of work that not only formally contradict the stylistic consistency and monochromatic
palette of the Butterfly abstractions but add tremendously to their content. These bodies
of work reveal an artist of broad interests and influences who has been deftly juggling
conflicting artistic sensibilities for years. When these are viewed alongside his equally
diverse range of works on paper, one gets a sense of the intensely scattered approach of
his creative search, calling to mind Anton Ehrenzweig's description of a genuinely creative
process: "to say that the creative mind is indifferent to the final outcome obscures the real
issue. The creative searcher is, of course, extremely concerned about the effect his interim
decisions might have on the end result, but he must be able to bear the suspense."[1]

Certain patterns and connections that have emerged thus far in Grotjahn's work offer
clues to his practice. One is a tendency toward opposition: in numerous ways, the artist
pushes his work forward by making one sort of statement and then contradicting it, something that happens within a single canvas as well as between different paintings. In the
Butterfly series, for instance, the evidence of authorial activity is plainly seen in the luscious
oil-on-linen brushwork, but that vitality is reined in by the strict geometry of the compositions.
Flourishes of the hand are confined to the signatures he imposes on the paintings, but in
reality the signatures exist as absences, areas that the brush has consciously avoided,
leaving the underpainting to shine through. The visual references the paintings make are
also at odds with one another, conjuring the seriousness of early Frank Stella stripe
paintings while deflating it with the gaudy and overly self-aggrandizing signatures and
dates. In addition, his compositional schemes and additive method of filling in recall the
doodles of a bored student, but Grotjahn elevates these techniques to the status of high art
with expensive oils and beautifully crafted supports.

Greater antagonism exists between individual canvases that share the walls in his
studio and receive his attention accordingly. One gets the sense that for one kind of painting

---

1. Anton Ehrenzweig, The Hidden Order of Art: A Study in the Psychology of Artistic Imagination
(Berkeley: University of California Press, 1967), 48.

to exist, another must also come into being as an antidote. While a Butterfly might look kooky next to a Stella, it looks positively Apollonian next to one of Grotjahn's Picassoid Face Paintings, in which striated flesh, flaring nostrils, and obsessive scarification approach Australian aboriginal art. The Faces tend to upend the transcendent purity of the abstractions through their manic energy. Compositionally similar to the Butterflies, they feature representational eyes, noses, and baboonlike wrinkles scratched onto abstract centrifugal structures. When he is not painting, Grotjahn is a consummate poker player, and he has drawn comparisons between his card-playing and his studio work. About his poker strategy, he explained he will "occasionally play questionable hands to mix it up or show the table that [he]'ll play the worst cards and bluff,"[2] an approach that one could see mirrored in the relationship between the winning Butterflies and almost outré Face Paintings.

If the discord between the Faces and the Butterflies gives Grotjahn room to move and explore, his Flower Paintings make it even harder to pin him down. These are done in a cartoonish hand, with clearly demarcated areas of color and simply outlined forms silhouetted on plain backgrounds. The Flowers are pointedly clumsy, done with seemingly unskilled brushwork and little ambition for draftsmanship, which is undercut further by the overlay of rudimentary smiling facial features. These pieces do in fact derive in part from another author—in this case, the artist's psychoanalyst grandfather, whose doodles and drawings of flowers and other subject matter Grotjahn has been appropriating for several years. Grotjahn replicates and then counters his grandfather's style, which tends toward the illustrational, with a slacker-style roughness, sometimes going so far as to affix stuffed athletic socks to the canvases as graceless noses.

Grotjahn's taste for the abject is given even more play in another series of works fashioned out of cardboard boxes and toilet-paper tubes. The slapdash Masks resemble the Faces and Flowers but establish an even less polished aesthetic pole—one that is equal parts gradeschool craft project and shantytown shamanism. The Masks, as quasi-functional disguises, imply a performative aspect that is subtly echoed in the task-oriented processes behind the poker playing, the creation of the Butterflies, and his ongoing Sign-Exchange

2. Mark Grotjahn, in conversation with the author, Los Angeles, 19 January 2005.

project—processes not often found in a typical painting practice but that give the artist license to explore different modes of expression.

The Sign-Exchange project reveals Grotjahn's appreciation of the more mundane function of painting: handpainted signs that business owners make. Long attracted by the directness and unpretentiousness of these signs, coupled with their often surprising visual ingenuity, he conducted a project in which he replicated signs he saw around his neighborhood and then traded his versions with shop owners for the originals, exhibiting them alongside his canvases. In addition to the obvious connections to the Flower Paintings derived from his grandfather's drawings, this project is crucial to understanding his work as a whole, for the entire range of painting's communicative possibilities fascinates him and warrants inclusion in his work. The Butterflies are just as tied to the decorative conventions of low-tech sign painting as they are to high modernist discourse, and the leap from a roughshod Mask to a powerful aggressive Face simply demonstrates the complexity of his sensibilities. Grotjahn has said that the range of work he has undertaken thus far represents "different parts of his personality and different kinds of art [he] likes."[3] By opening up his practice to such a range of potential influences, he has set the stage for an endless and ambitious diversification of his work.

3. Ibid.

WORKS IN THE EXHIBITION

Selections from Untitled (Mask) series,
2002–04
Acrylic on cardboard boxes
Dimensions variable
Collection of the artist, Los Angeles

UNTITLED (WEDDING MASK—ANCHOR STEAM),
2002–04
Acrylic on cardboard box
16 1/2 x 11 1/2 x 12 1/2 inches
Collection of the artist, Los Angeles

UNTITLED (WEDDING MASK—BASS), 2002–04
Acrylic on cardboard box
15 x 10 x 16 inches
Collection of the artist, Los Angeles

UNTITLED (WEDDING MASK—NEWCASTLE), 2002–04
Acrylic on cardboard box
15 x 10 1/4 x 12 3/4 inches
Collection of the artist, Los Angeles

UNTITLED (WEDDING MASK—PERONI), 2002–04
Acrylic on cardboard box
15 x 10 1/4 x 13 inches
Collection of the artist, Los Angeles

UNTITLED (WEDDING MASK—SPATEN), 2002–04
Acrylic on cardboard box
16 x 10 3/4 x 14 inches
Collection of the artist, Los Angeles

UNTITLED (GREEN BUTTERFLY M. GROTJAHN 03), 2003
Oil on linen
69 x 54 inches
Collection of David and Tia Hoberman,
Los Angeles

UNTITLED (ANGRY FLOWER), 2004
Oil, enamel paint, and mixed media on canvas
89 x 60 inches
Collection of David Teiger

UNTITLED (BLACK BUTTERFLY OVER GREEN), 2004
Oil on linen
70 x 35 inches
Collection of the artist, Los Angeles

UNTITLED (FACE), 2004
Oil on cardboard
42 x 33 inches
Collection of the artist, Los Angeles

UNTITLED (FACE), 2004
Oil on cardboard
24 x 18 inches
Collection of the artist, Los Angeles

UNTITLED (FACE), 2004
Oil on cardboard
19 x 17 inches
Collection of the artist, Los Angeles

UNTITLED, 2005
Oil on canvas
58 x 48 inches
Collection of Rosa and Carlos de la Cruz,
Miami

UNTITLED (FLOWER), 2005
Oil on cardboard
43 x 27 inches
Collection of the artist, Los Angeles

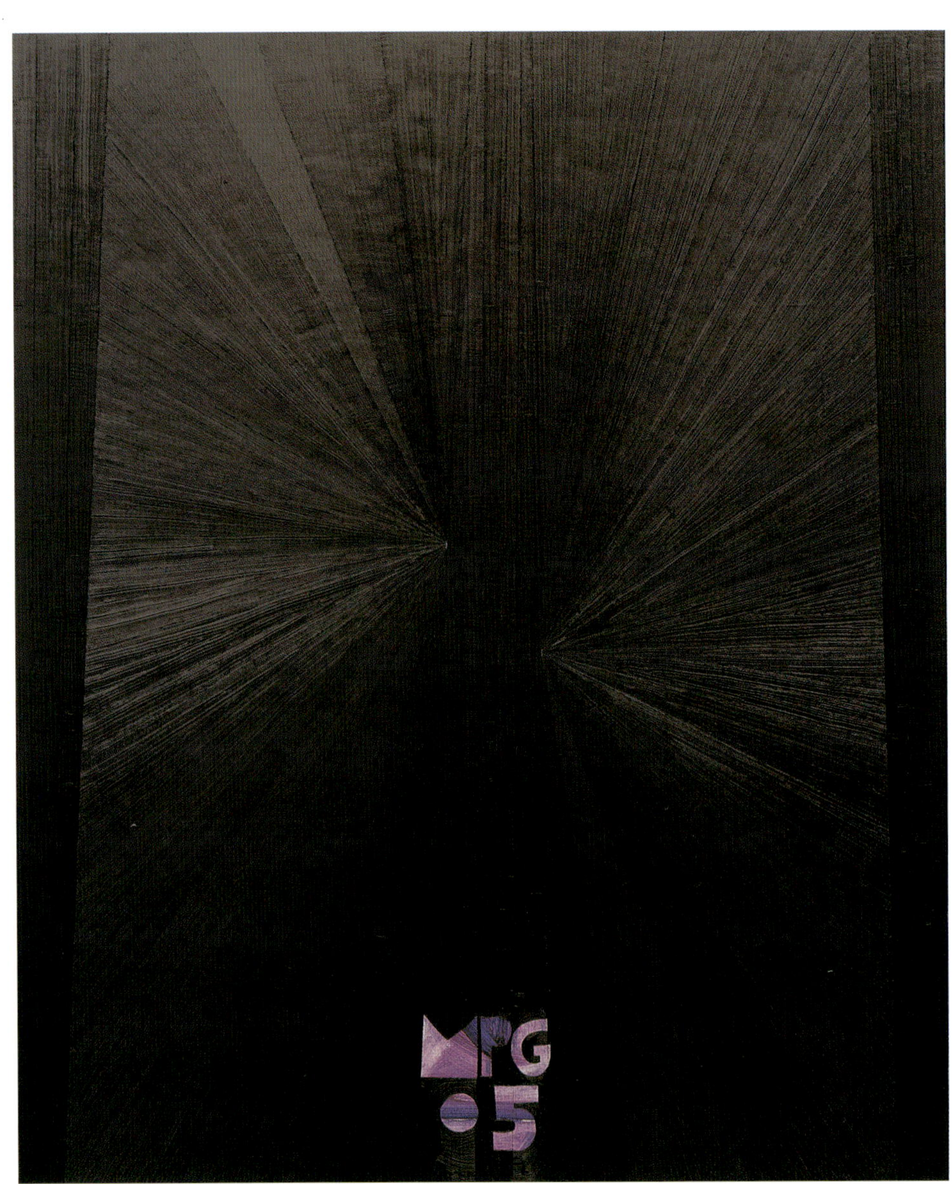

UNTITLED (BLACK BUTTERFLY DIOXIDE MPG05), 2005
Oil on linen
58 x 48 inches
Collection of Frank Cohen, Manchester, England

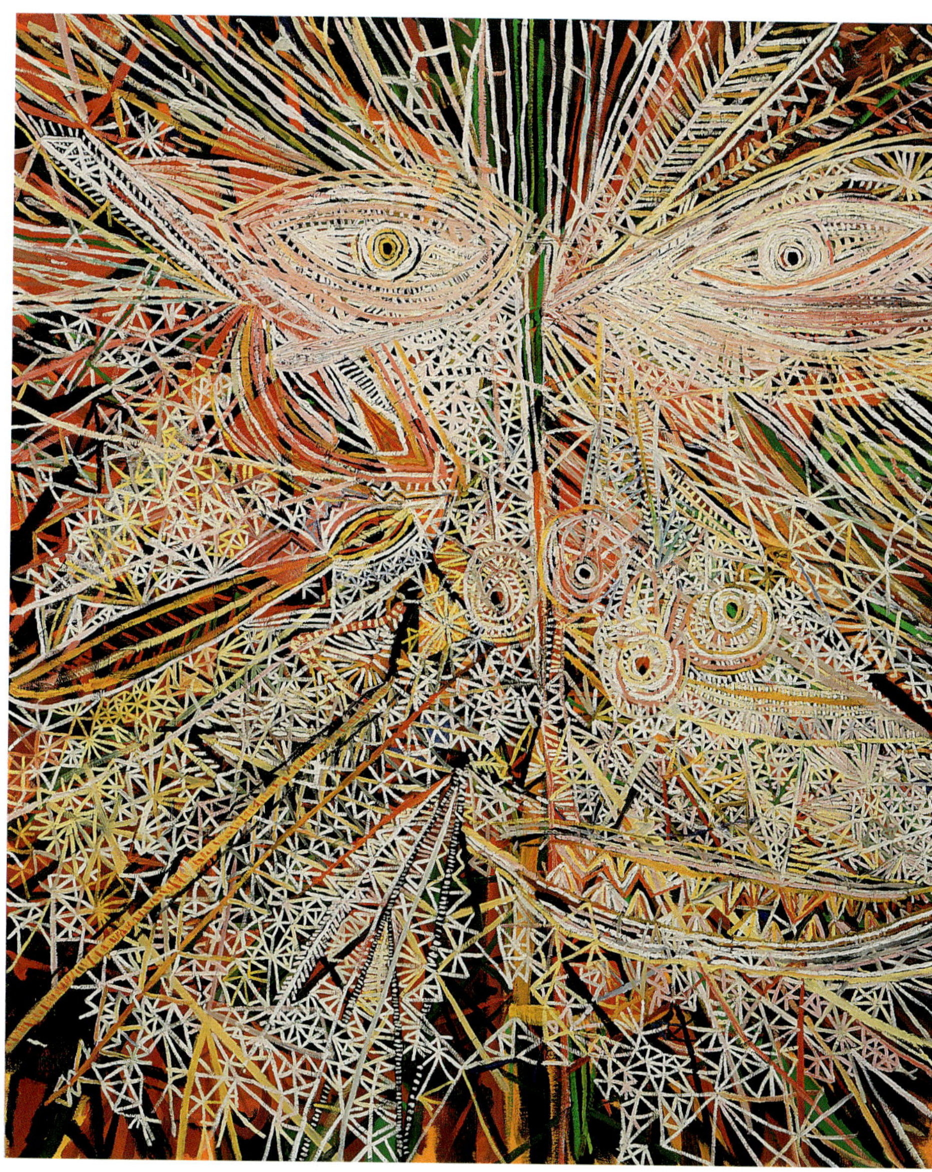

UNTITLED, 2005
Oil on canvas
58 x 48 inches
Collection of Rosa and Carlos de la Cruz, Miami

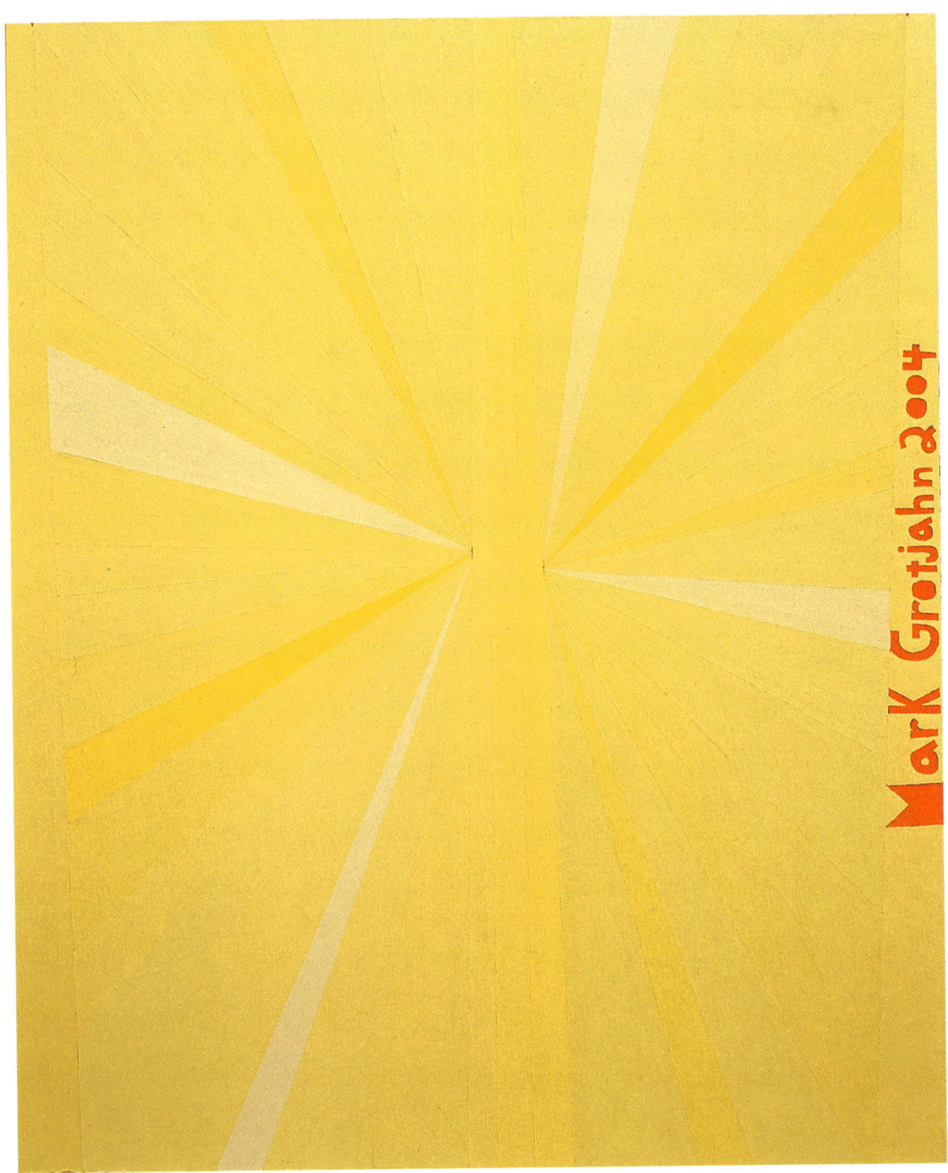

UNTITLED (YELLOW BUTTERFLY ORANGE MARK GROTJAHN 2004), 2004
Oil on linen
60 x 50 inches
Collection of David Teiger

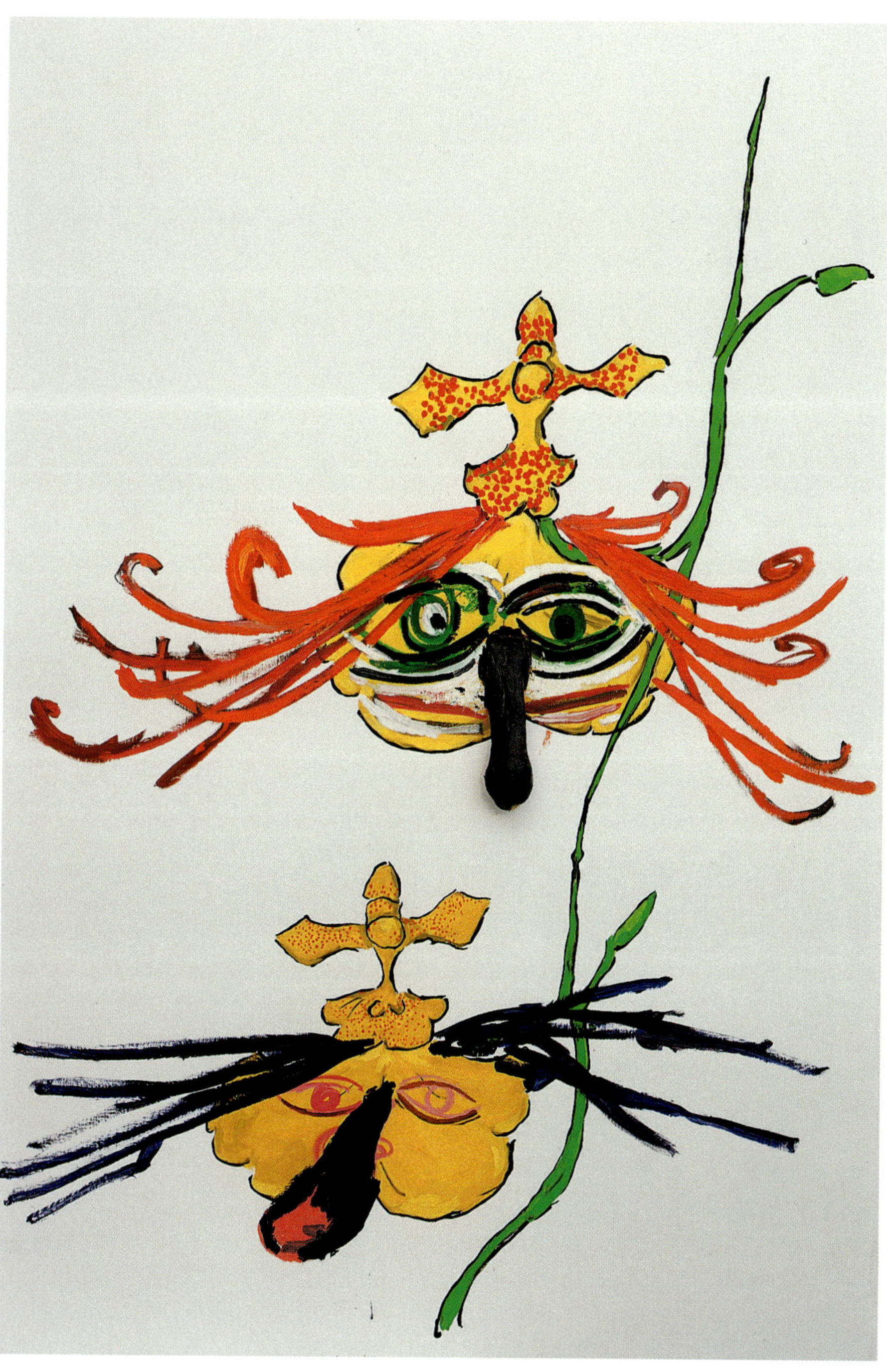

UNTITLED (ANGRY FLOWER), 2004
Oil, enamel paint, and mixed media on canvas
89 x 60 inches
Collection of David Teiger

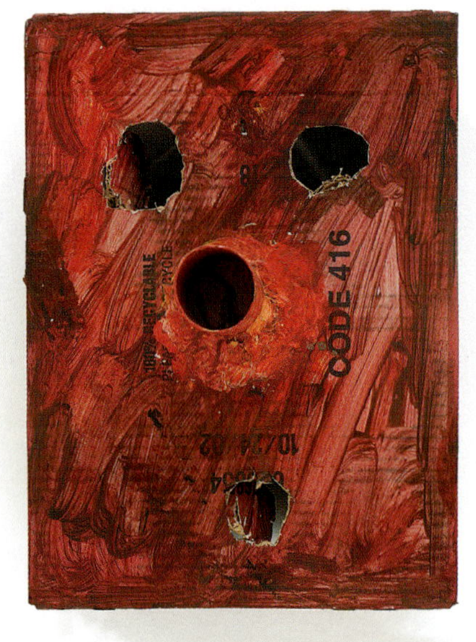

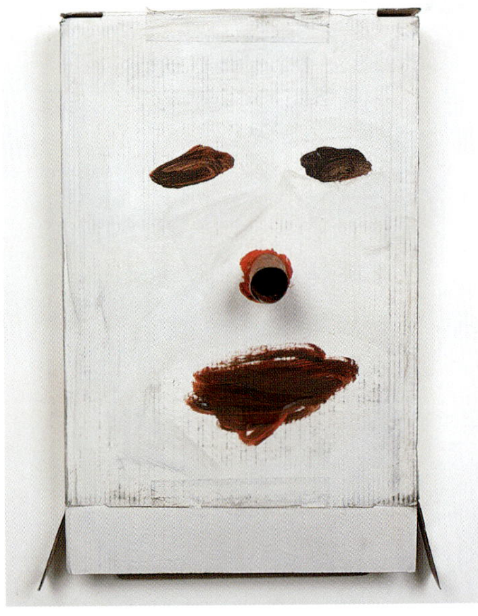

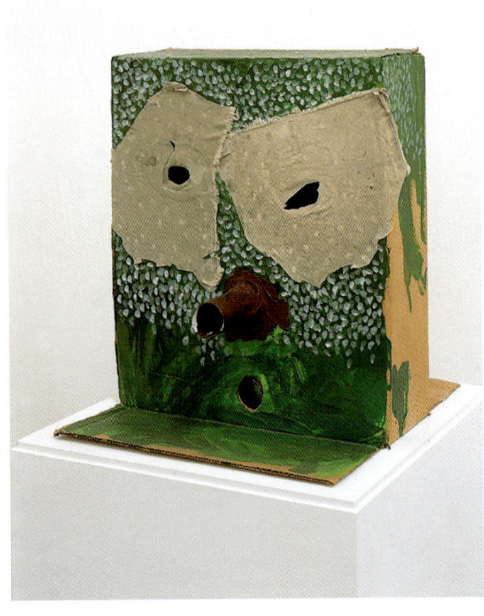

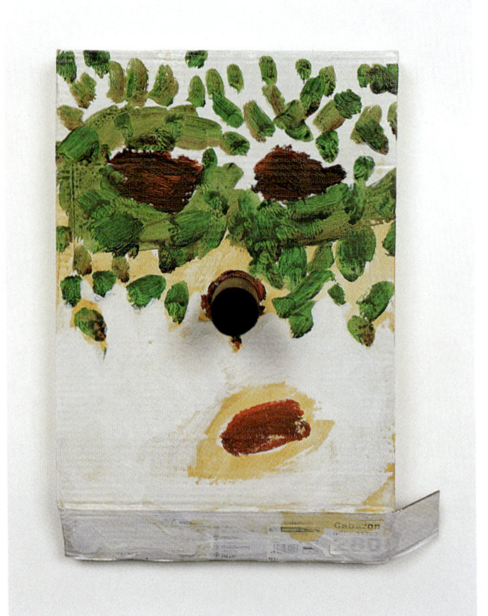

Top left:
UNTITLED (RED MASK), 2004
Acrylic on cardboard box
14 x 11 x 8 inches
Collection of the artist, Los Angeles

Details from Untitled (Mask) series, 2002–04
Acrylic on cardboard boxes
Dimensions variable
Collection of the artist, Los Angeles

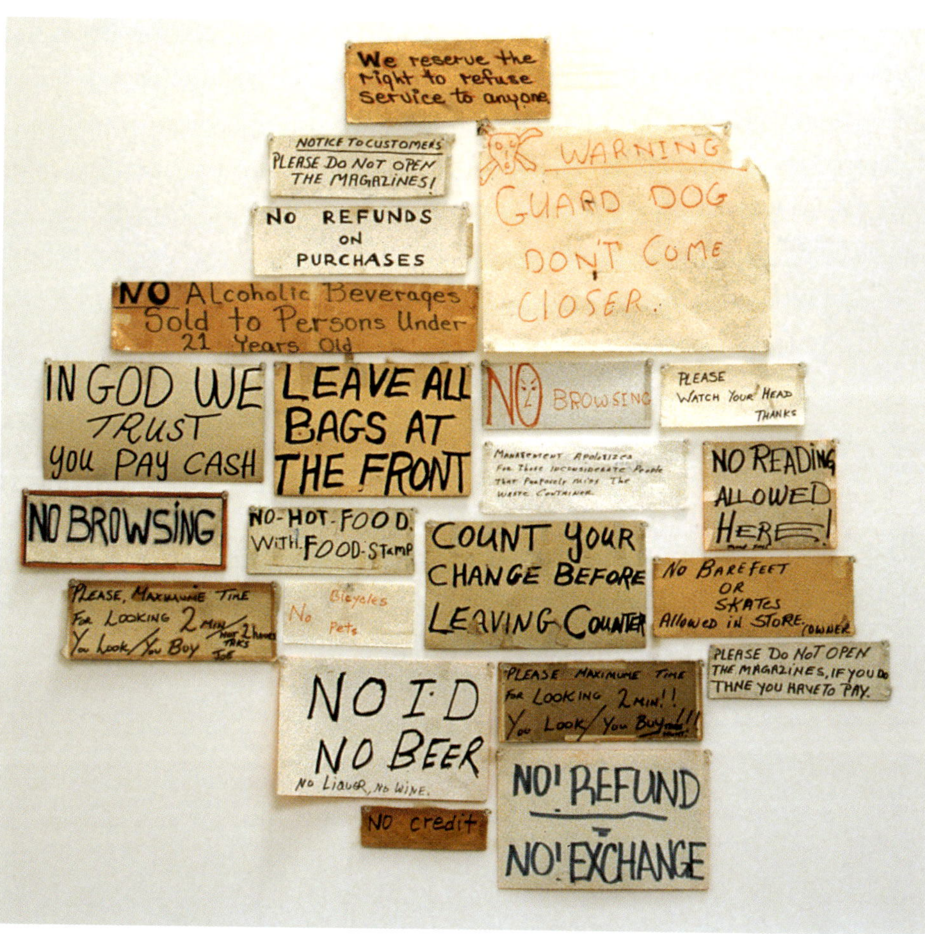

NO, NO, NO, 1994–95
Pen on paper
67 x 62 inches
Collection of Gaby and Wilhelm Schürmann, Aachen, Germany

Lucy McKenzie in her studio, Glasgow, Scotland
Still from McKenzie and Paulina Olowska, OBLIQUE COMPOSITION III, 2003, video, 10 minutes, courtesy of
the artists and Cabinet, London

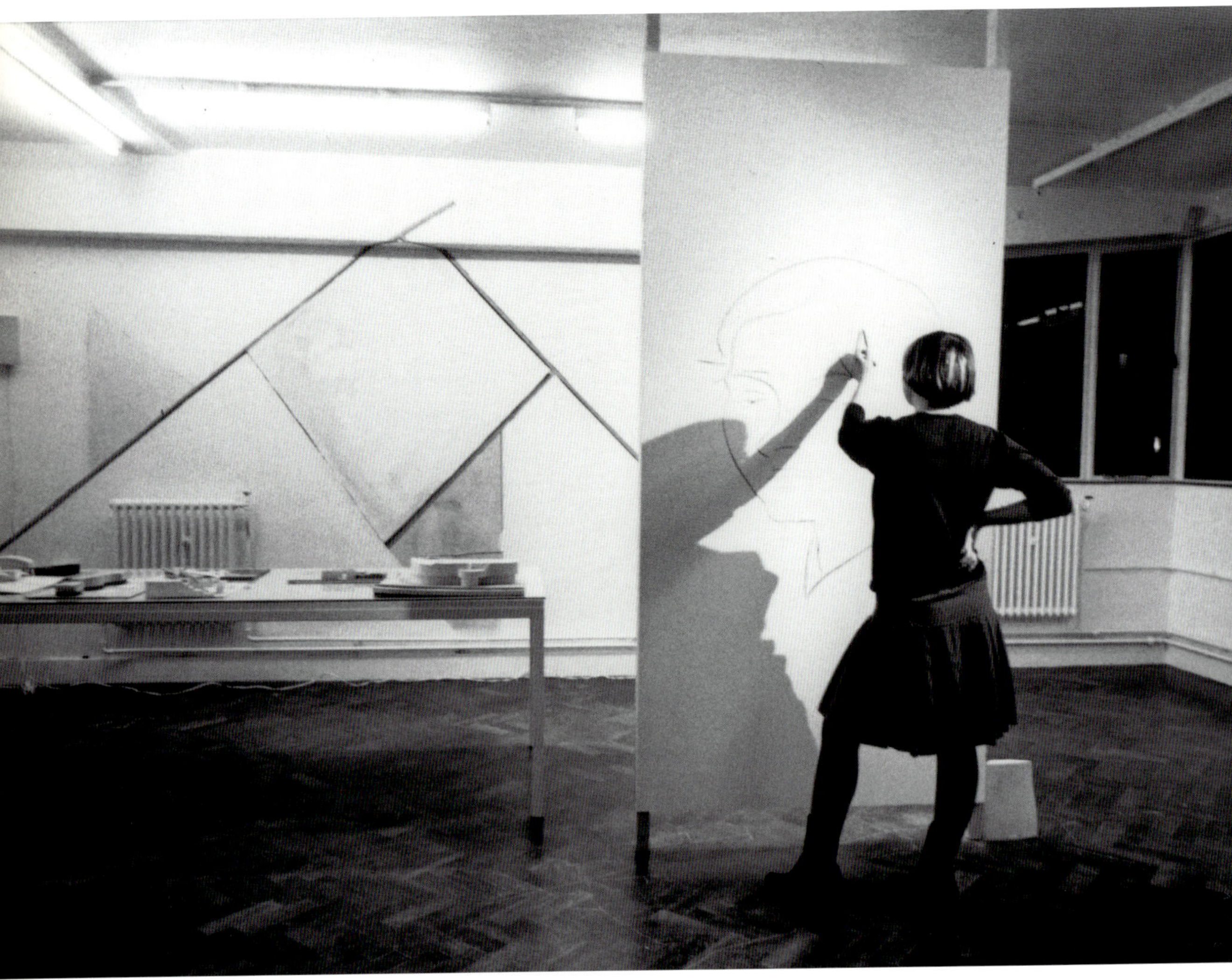

b. 1977, Glasgow, Scotland;
lives in Glasgow

Selected Solo and Two-Person Exhibitions

2005 "Smersh," Metro Pictures, New York
2004 "Deathwatch," Van Abbemuseum, Eindhoven,
     The Netherlands (exh. cat.)
     Cabinet, London
     "Kulaks," Galerie Daniel Buchholz,
     Cologne, Germany
     The Institute of Contemporary Art, Boston
2003 "Brian Eno," Neuer Aachener Kunst-
     verein, Aachen, Germany (exh. cat.)
     "Nova Popularna" (collaboration with
     Paulina Olowska), site-specific project,
     Foksal Gallery Foundation, Warsaw (exh. cat.)
2002 "Art Now: Lucy McKenzie," Tate Britain,
     London
     "If It Moves, Kiss It," Galerie Christian
     Nagel, Berlin
2001 "Global Joy," Galerie Daniel Buchholz,
     Cologne, Germany (exh. cat.)
2000 "Decemberism," Cabinet, London

Selected Group Exhibitions

2003 25th International Biennial of Graphic
     Arts, Cankarjev Dom, Ljubljana
     (exh. cat.)
     "Dreams and Conflicts: The Dictatorship
     of the Viewer," Venice Biennale,
     Venice, Italy (exh. cat.)
2002 "Kontext, Form, Troja," Secession,
     Vienna (exh. cat.)
     "Painting on the Move," Kunsthalle,
     Basel, Switzerland (exh. cat.)
2001 "Painting at the Edge of the World,"
     Walker Art Center, Minneapolis
     (exh. cat.)
2000 Beck's Futures, Institute for Contem-
     porary Arts, London; Cornerhouse,
     Manchester, England; and Centre for
     Contemporary Arts, Glasgow, Scotland
1999 "Village Disco," Cabinet, London

Lucy McKenzie

Painting in Tongues

Selected Bibliography

- Archer, Michael. "Lucy McKenzie."
Artforum 40, no. 1 (September 2001): 184–85.
- Farquharson, Alex. "Lucy McKenzie at
Cabinet Gallery." Art Monthly, no. 243
(February 2001): 35–37.
- Graw, Isabelle. "A Star Is Born." Texte
zur Kunst, no. 44 (December 2001): 171–75.
Review of Galerie Daniel Buchholz exhibition.
- Kempkes, Anke. "Lucy McKenzie at Galerie
Daniel Buchholz." Translated by Helen Slater.
Frieze, no. 63 (November–December 2001):
122–23.
- Mulholland, Neil. "Lucy McKenzie." Flash
Art, no. 219 (July–September 2001): 115.
- Ruf, Beatrix. "Lucy McKenzie." In Cream,
200–03. London: Phaidon Press, 2003.
- Slyce, John. "Lucy McKenzie at Cabinet
Gallery." Artext, no. 73 (May–July 2001): 88.

In the relatively short time that Lucy McKenzie has been exhibiting her work, she has already established herself with a wide-ranging and ambitious oeuvre that includes painting, works on paper, installation, video, murals, performance, writing, and even a record label. Painting remains primary to her artistic endeavor—in particular, how painting functions in the public realm. In that regard, her work often takes into account the context in which it is to be shown and how it can embody a sense of agency. In responding to different sites, McKenzie has incorporated a broad palette of styles and techniques, while her subject matter remains relatively constant. McKenzie's work can in fact appear almost anonymous at times, slyly blending in with its surroundings while simultaneously engaging in critique.

For instance, her 2004 installation Deathwatch at the Van Abbemuseum in Eindhoven, The Netherlands, included a mural installed in a hallway and on an adjacent outdoor wall that links the museum to its café. Within the hallway McKenzie installed brick-patterned wallpaper on which she painted trompe l'oeil figures and ersatz artworks that appeared to be hanging on or displayed in front of this "brick" wall. The non-accessible glassed-in wall, which curves around an outdoor pool, was decorated with inoffensive geometric compositions that ape well-meaning neighborhood beautification schemes. Together, the two segments created a parallel reality that depicted art in commune with its public while simultaneously conducting a real-time dialogue between artwork and viewer. Figure and ground, past and present were provocatively intertwined, attempting to reconcile what the artist called her "dissatisfactions with art representing life."[1]

Murals hold particular fascination for McKenzie, especially publicly sanctioned ones that seem to express collective ideals. In a 2004 lecture, she mentioned her curiosity about how murals attempt to "encapsulate the problems of the world in a waving child or a dove."[2] This was the basis for an ambitious public project in Gdansk, Poland, called Plastyczna Integracja (2001), in which she and her regular collaborator Paulina Olowska painted a long wall with a panoply of common mural tropes, from abstract supergraphics to socialist-realist figure groups and traditional architectural motifs.

1. Lucy McKenzie, in Journal #5: Lucy McKenzie—Deathwatch, exh. brochure (Eindhoven, The Netherlands: Van Abbemuseum, 2004), 6.

2. McKenzie, in a lecture at the Institute of Contemporary Art, Boston, 22 September 2004.

The public's ambivalence during the work's realization was immensely interesting to the artists, as were the subsequent (uninvited) additions made to the work by local graffiti taggers. The defacement of murals was the subject of two near-twin canvases from 2002, both untitled. One shows a side view of a human brain being carefully painted onto a dilapidated plaster wall by a young woman, and the other shows the same woman painting a stylized graphic of the word "brain" onto a wall while being victimized herself by crude graffiti. Between the two, one is made aware of the gap between representation and reality and also reminded of the truly active and even democratic sphere in which public art exists.

The power public artwork can have in its civic context—referred to as its "actuality" by McKenzie—has also been taken up in recent pieces, with subject matter and site-specificities guiding her visual language. One such work, Co? Ne! (2004), is a study for a mural the artist proposed for the side of a building in Düsseldorf, Germany. The artist borrowed stylistic cues from bygone commercial precedents to create a fictional deodorant advertisement, replete with nonsensical text. The image—which features a liberated bikini-clad woman beguiling her male entourage to the point that they eat her serpentine armpit hair—is a bizarre extension of Women's Lib iconography and is better understood as a canny blending of advertising, political propaganda, and graffiti conventions. How it would settle with its neighbors in a newly gentrified harbor area if it were rendered at full scale will never be tested, but it is clearly designed to raise questions and eyebrows rather than assuage its public with soothing or pleasing imagery the way conventional advertising does. McKenzie's take on public art is by no means fixed or one-sided, as can be seen in an untitled 2005 canvas in which a woman is so visibly oppressed by the blatantly sexual image hanging on the ornate café wall behind her that she is barely able to eat her meal. This scene was based on an experience the artist had at an upscale restaurant where one of Jeff Koons's pornographic Made in Heaven pictures loomed aggressively over her head. She substituted an erotic cartoon by Italian artist Milo Manara with Flemish text, embellishing the background with richly marbled surfaces, flaunting her recently acquired command of faux finishes as well as her knack for photorealistic portraiture in her treatment of the woman. Though this work is vastly different in execution and style from Co? Ne!, the two are nevertheless linked to other equally dissimilar pieces in her oeuvre by their overarching thematic consideration of art's potential to affect and engage the spaces it inhabits, whether actively or passively.

WORKS IN THE EXHIBITION

AESTHETIC INTEGRATION POLAND, 2001
Linoprint with collage
17 x 12 inches
Courtesy Galerie Daniel Buchholz, Cologne

AESTHETIC INTEGRATION SCOTLAND, 2001
Linoprint with collage
17 x 12 inches
Courtesy Galerie Daniel Buchholz, Cologne

GLOBAL JOY, 2001
Mixed media on linoprint
Ten works: 17 x 12 inches each
Various lenders

GLOBAL JOY IV, 2001
Linoprint
12 x 16 3/4 inches
Courtesy Galerie Daniel Buchholz, Cologne

Lucy McKenzie and Paulina Olowska
Source material for PLASTYCZNA INTEGRACJA,
2001
Photographs and drawings
Dimensions variable
Collection of the artists, Glasgow and
Krakow

Source material for OPTIMISM/PESSIMISM, 2002
Mixed media
Dimensions variable
Collection of the artist, Glasgow

SUBTROPEN MAGAZINE, 2002
Newsprint
Dimensions variable
Collection of the artist, Glasgow

Lucy McKenzie and Paulina Olowska
NOVA POPULARNA, 2004
LP record
12 x 12 inches
The Museum of Contemporary Art, Los Angeles,
Library Collection

Source material for NOVA POPULARNA, 2003
Mixed media on paper
Dimensions variable
Collection of the artist, Glasgow

UNTITLED, 2004
Oil on canvas
96 x 72 inches
The Institute of Contemporary Art, Boston
Promised gift of David Teiger

UNTITLED (BI-CURIOUS), 2004
Oil and collage on canvas
96 x 72 inches
Private collection, Germany
Courtesy Cabinet, London

UNTITLED (BI-CURIOUS), 2004
Acrylic and collage on paper
12 x 8 3/4 inches
Collection of Sarah Staton, London
Courtesy of Cabinet, London

Source material for DEATHWATCH, 2004
Photographs and sketches
Dimensions variable
Collection of the artist, Glasgow

CHEYNEY AND EILEEN DISTURB A HISTORIAN
AT POMPEII, 2005
Acrylic and ink on paper
100 x 136 inches
Courtesy of the artist and Metro Pictures,
New York

Source material for CHEYNEY AND EILEEN
DISTURB A HISTORIAN AT POMPEII, 2005
Mixed media on paper
Dimensions variable
Collection of the artist, Glasgow

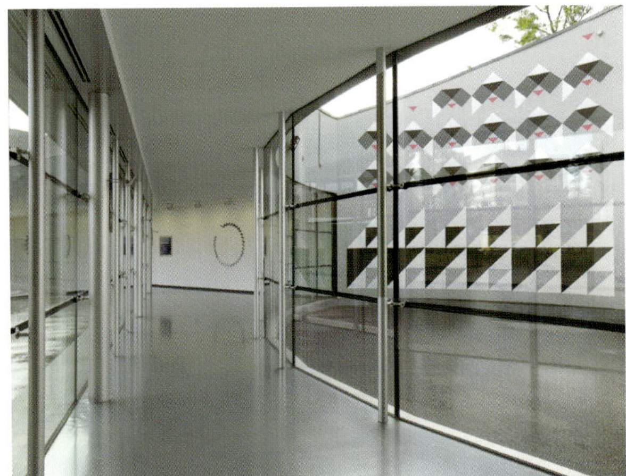

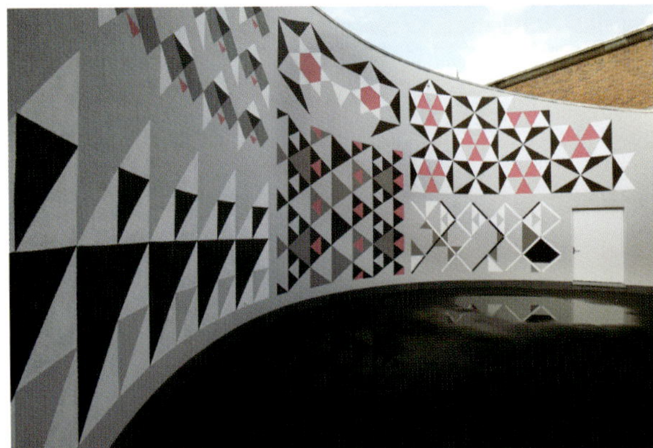

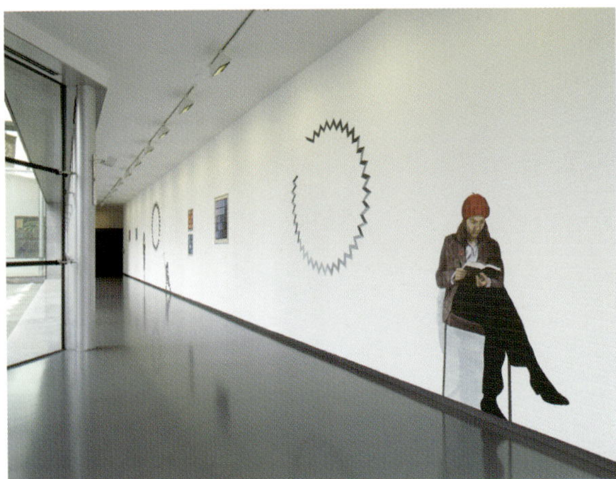

Details of DEATHWATCH, 2004
DVD projection, acrylic wall painting on MDF panels, and fake-brick wallpaper
Mural dimensions: 10 x 75 7/8 feet overall
Installation at Van Abbemuseum, Eindhoven, The Netherlands, 2004

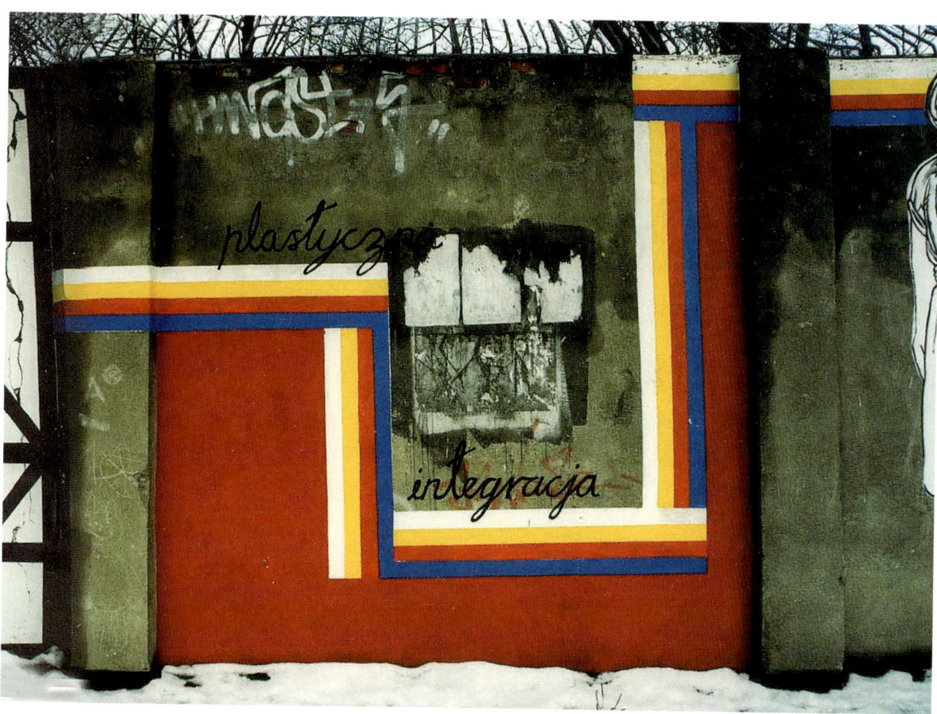

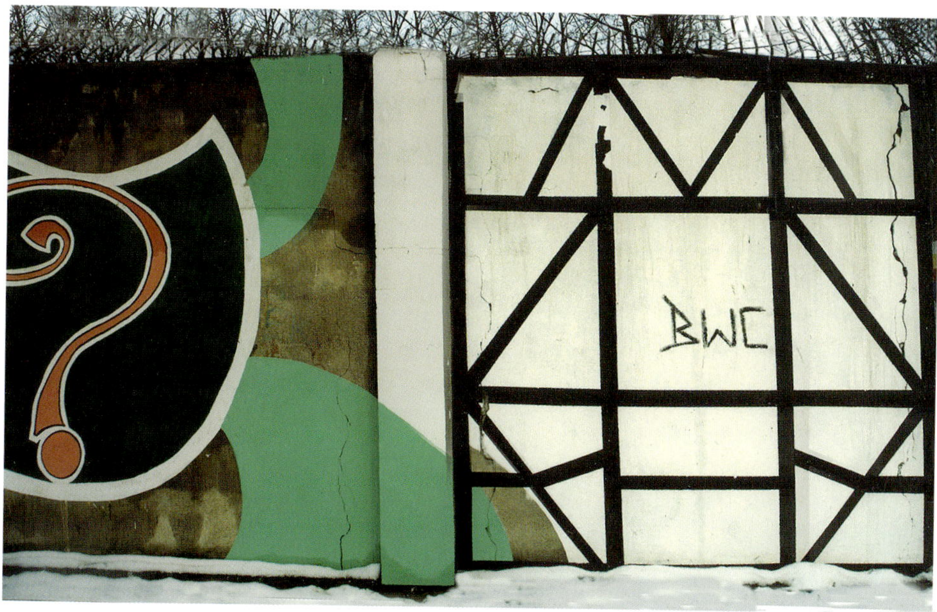

Lucy McKenzie and Paulina Olowska
Details of PLASTYCZNA INTEGRACJA, 2001
Acrylic and mixed media on wall
Approximately 328 feet
Installation at Festiwal Malarstwa Sciennego, Kliniczna, Gdansk, Poland, 2001

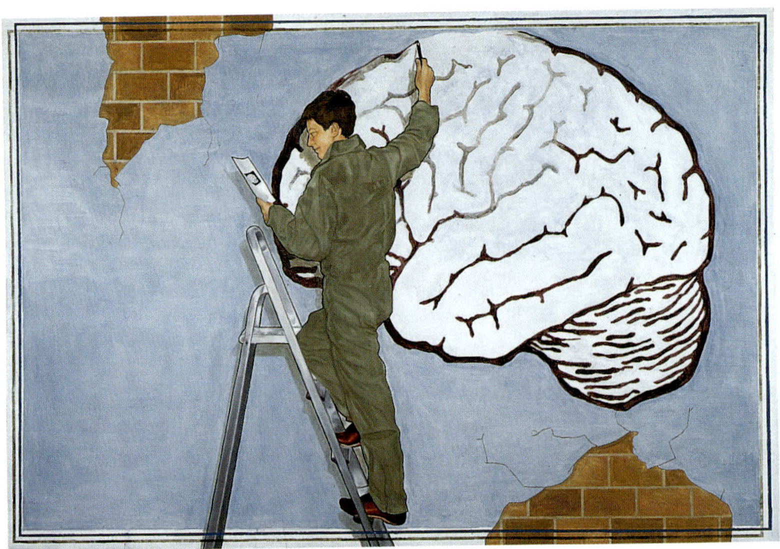

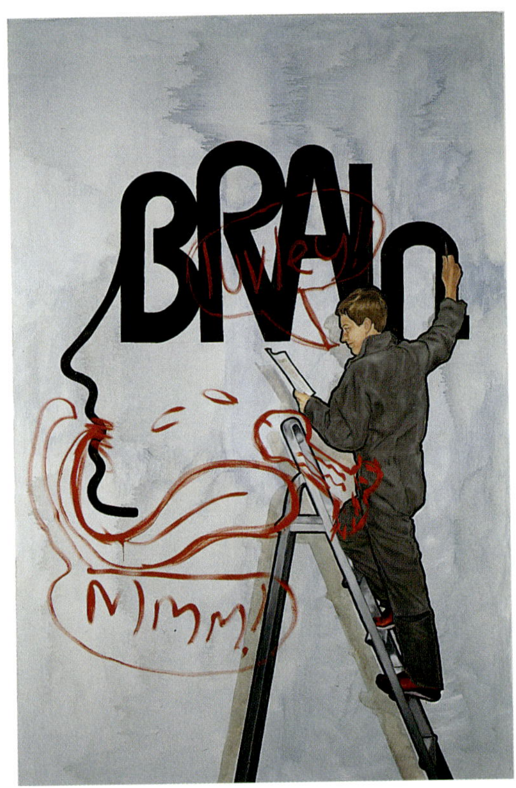

Top:
UNTITLED, 2002
Acrylic and oil on canvas
78 3/4 x 118 1/8 inches
Courtesy Cabinet, London

Bottom:
UNTITLED, 2002
Acrylic and oil on canvas
118 1/8 x 78 3/4 inches
Courtesy Galerie Daniel Buchholz, Cologne

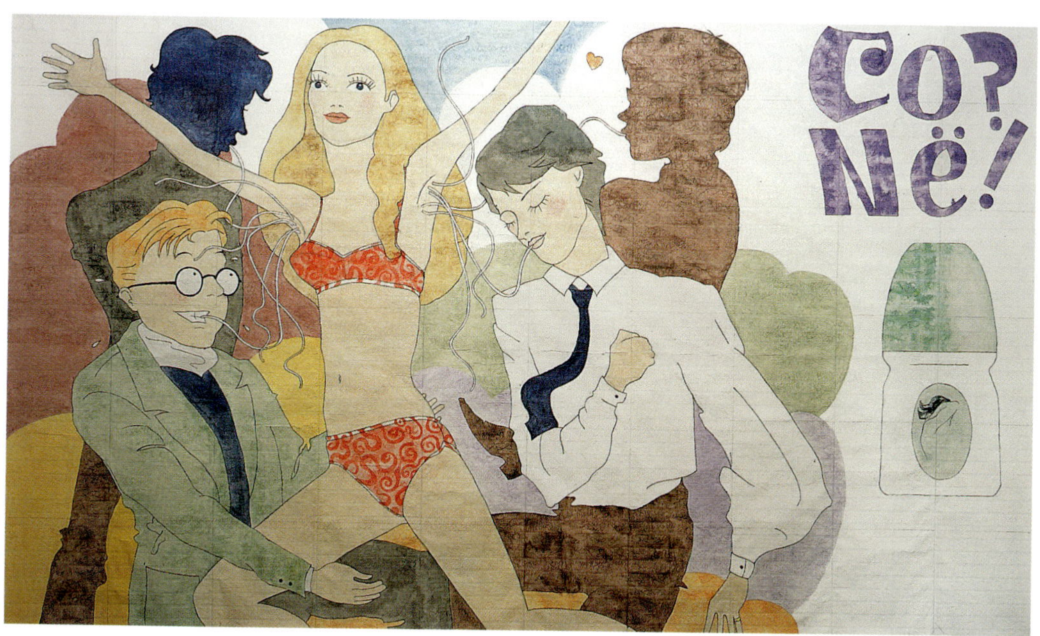

CO? NE!, 2004
Acrylic and pencil on wallpaper
137 13/16 x 208 11/16 inches
Private collection, Italy

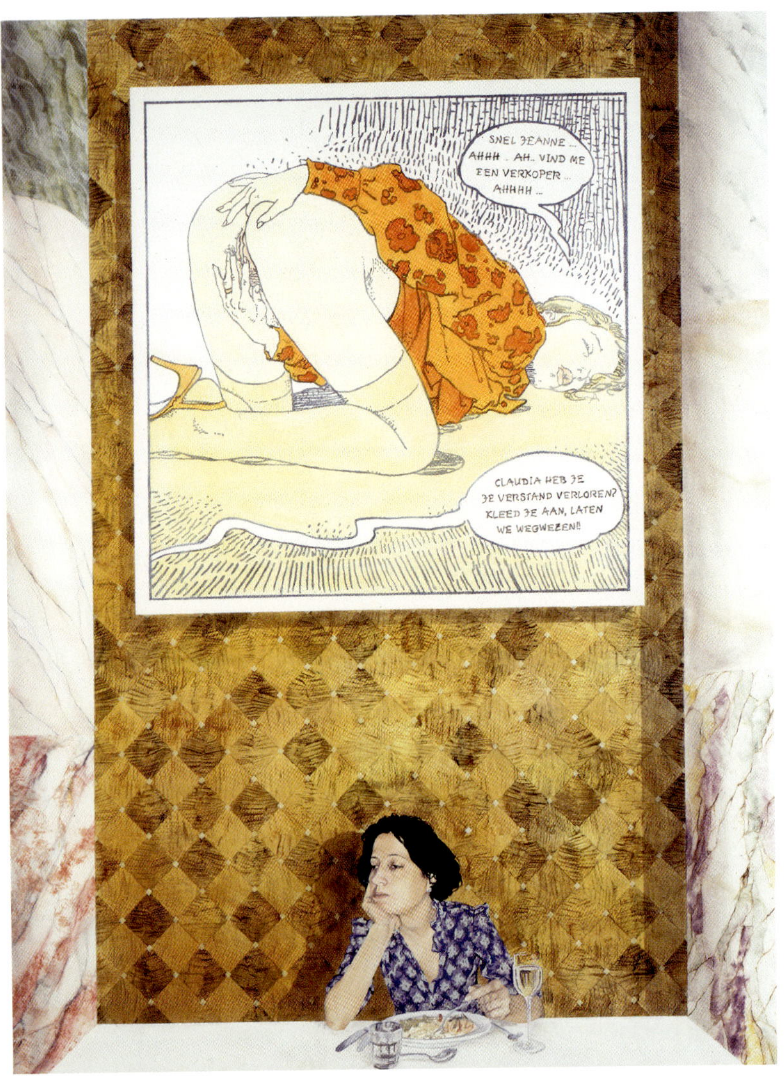

UNTITLED, 2005
Oil on canvas
72 1/4 x 96 1/16 inches
Courtesy of the artist and Metro Pictures, New York

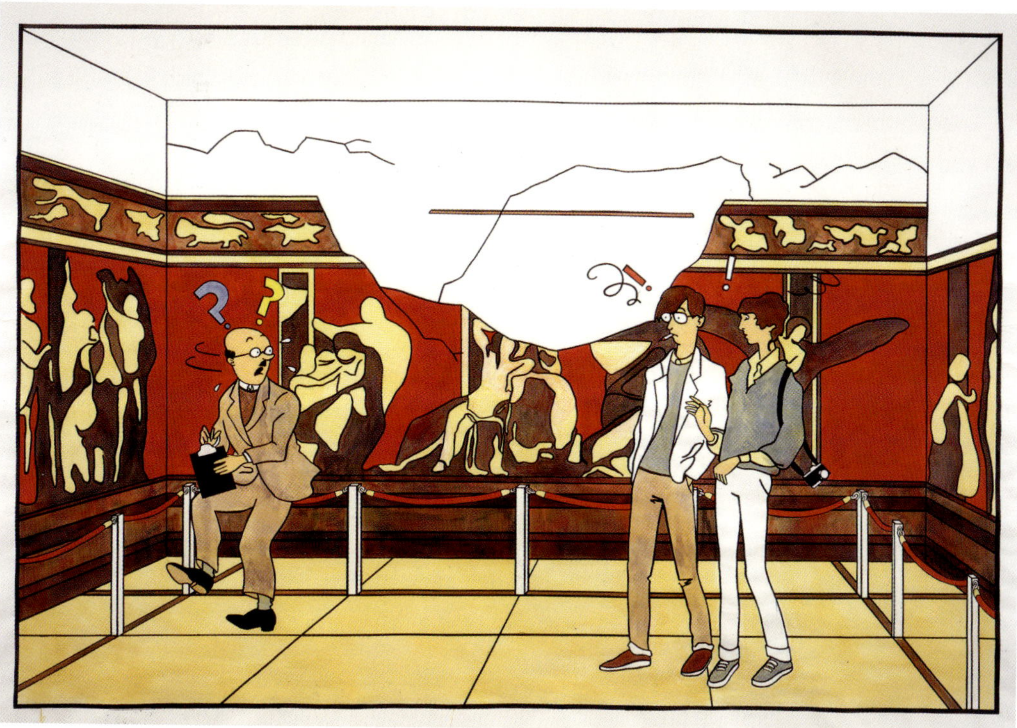

CHEYNEY AND EILEEN DISTURB A HISTORIAN AT POMPEII, 2005
Acrylic and ink on paper
100 x 136 inches
Courtesy of the artist and Metro Pictures, New York

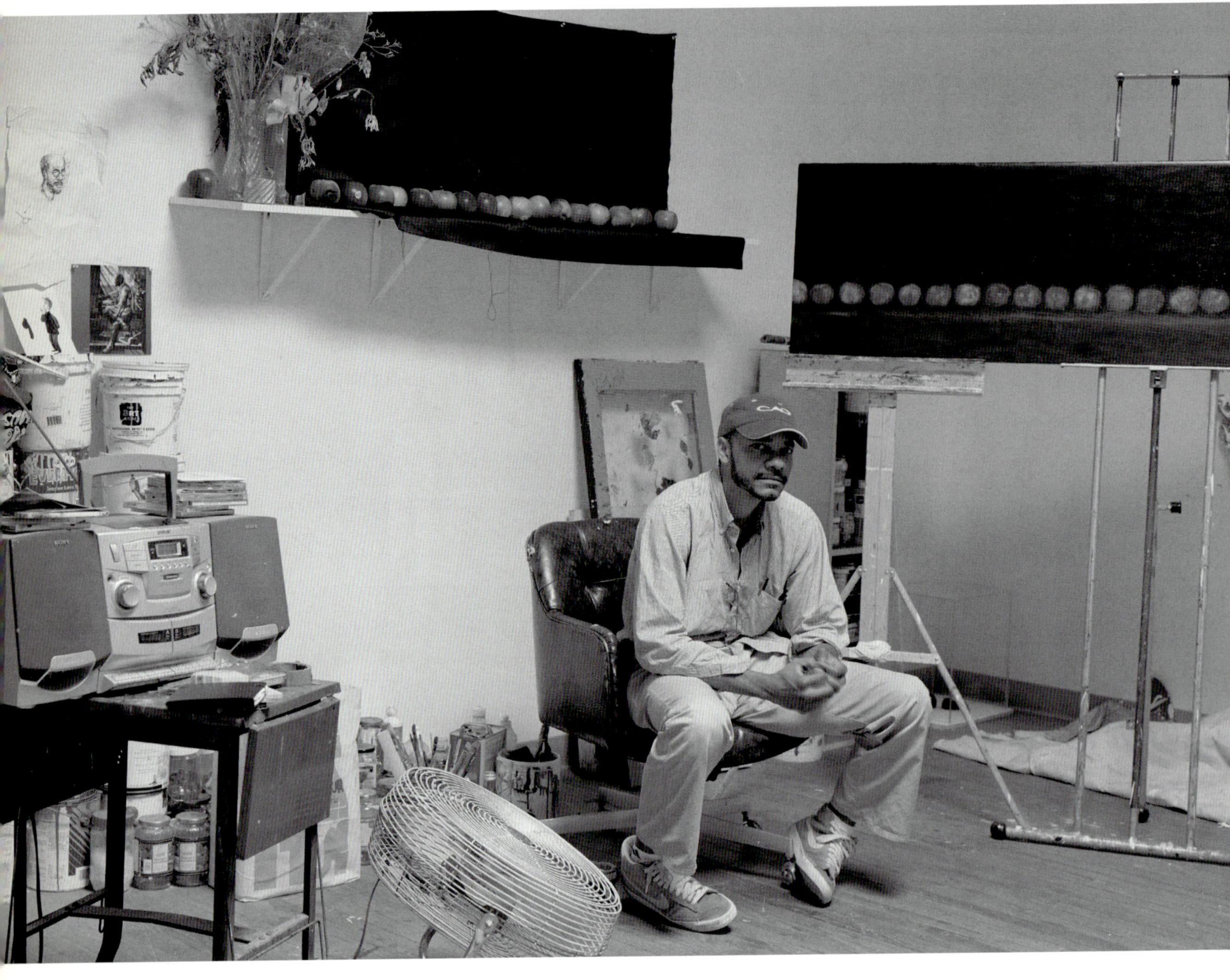

b. 1969, Columbia, South Carolina;
lives in Los Angeles

Selected Solo and Two-Person Exhibitions

2005 "Untitled (ellipses) III," Triple
Candie, New York
Galleria Estro, Padua, Italy
2004 "On Comfort," Adamski Gallery for
Contemporary Art, Aachen, Germany
"New" (collaboration with Edgar
Arceneaux), Susanne Vielmetter
Los Angeles Projects, Los Angeles
2003 "Untitled (ellipses) II," Susanne
Vielmetter Los Angeles Projects,
Los Angeles
2002 "Untitled," Adamski Gallery for
Contemporary Art, Aachen, Germany
"Untitled," Finesilver Gallery,
San Antonio, Texas

Selected Group Exhibitions

2005 "Thing: New Sculpture from Los Angeles,"
Hammer Museum, Los Angeles
2004 "White Noise," Gallery at REDCAT,
Los Angeles
"Central Station: Collection Harald
Falckenberg," La Maison Rouge/
Foundation Antoine de Galbert, Paris
"Now Is a Good Time," Andrea Rosen
Gallery, New York
"FADE (1990–2003): African-American
Artists in Los Angeles—A Survey
Exhibition," Luckman Gallery and
University Fine Arts Gallery,
California State University, Los Angeles
2003 "Gibt's mich wirklich—Vier Räume aus
der Sammlung Schürmann," K21 Kunst-
sammlung Nordrhein-Westfalen,
Düsseldorf, Germany

Rodney McMillian

Painting in Tongues

"Veni Vidi Video," The Studio Museum
Harlem, New York
"Urban Aesthetics," California African
American Museum, Los Angeles
2002 "Messy Fingers: CalArts Graduate
Exhibition," Track 16, Santa Monica,
California

Selected Bibliography

- Harvey, Doug. "Color Theory: 'Fade' to
Black." L.A. Weekly (13–19 February 2004): 55.
Review of Luckman Gallery exhibition.
- Knight, Christopher. "A Chronicle of Race,
Rage, Ritual." Los Angeles Times, 17 February
2004.
- Myers, Holly. "Disposable Society." Los Angeles
Times, 13 October 2004. Review of REDCAT
exhibition.
- Myers, Julian. "Edgar Arceneaux and Rodney
McMillian." Frieze, no. 83 (May 2004): 92–93.

For Rodney McMillian, each painting summons a very specific and loaded history.
By actively pursuing a broad range of painterly activity—whether still life
or gestural abstraction—he activates a field of historical connotations and
stirs up questions about how consensus is built and histories are formed.
McMillian's art aims to open up canonized narratives to new interpretations.
The jarring segues from one work to another in his practice immediately spur
the viewer to make sense of his stylistic leaps, which in turn forces a closer
scrutiny of how individual works may be part of a greater system. McMillian
has recently begun conceiving of his exhibitions as sentences, with paintings
or other objects as the individual words.[1] Pull one word out of the sentence and
it may still be expressive, but it will lack cohesion and complexity.
McMillian's linguistic metaphor also asks the viewer to approach his paintings
in a rich poetic space, where "words" are measured against one another side by
side but also individually as part of a lengthy historical continuum.

The "words" McMillian works with tend to be packed with multivalent content that can be appreciated on a number of levels. For instance, the quality
of the artist's touch varies wildly from painting to painting, raising questions about the importance of mastery, skill, and craft. In still lifes such as
in progress (2003), paint has been handled deftly to create realistic-looking
books; whereas in Wood Paneling (2004), similarly realistic depictions of
nature have been commercially printed on thin sheets of veneered wood, which in
turn appear to have been salvaged from a demolition site. When these two works
are placed in relation to one another, the line of inquiry shifts to the personal history of the objects themselves—the former emerges as a commodity of
the kind aimed at the comfortable bourgeoisie for centuries, and the latter
a worthless relic. The conceptual friction generated by a side-by-side com-
parison of the two is precisely McMillian's intention, and it only increases as
other equally fraught artworks are introduced into the system.

1.   Rodney McMillian, in conversation with the author, Los Angeles, 7 February 2005.

Untitled (2002)—a large piece of vigorously worn, blue shag carpet that hangs on the wall—reveals no artistic intervention besides Duchampian selection, and yet it is commanding, meditative, and poignant, bringing a sense of its former life to the gallery. One art critic even found in it a "grandeur reminiscent of an Abstract Expressionist painting."[2] In another untitled work of 2004, McMillian utilized pours of paint reminiscent of Abstract Expressionism on an unstretched canvas attached haphazardly to the wall so that half of it remains on the floor, allowing footprints to accumulate. These challenges to notions of skill serve not only to interrogate the artist's own practice but to examine the propagation of aesthetic standards, which the artist believes are directly influenced by money and power.[3] McMillian's own skill is not actually at issue, as he clearly has a deft sense of composition and can handle paint well when he wants to, but he doesn't let us linger too long on special effects.

In a work such as Untitled (2003), McMillian highlights the historical privileging of one viewpoint over another by presenting a logical but unconventional way of seeing the world. Here, the upper half of an expanse of found dirty beige carpet is left untouched, while the bottom half is covered with a dynamic collage of magazine cutouts. The work inverts typical landscape conventions—the bare carpet suggesting terra firma and the cutouts representing a downward progression through strata of sky and space. This antipodal vision is obviously an affront to standard perception by upright gravity-bound beings but suggests an expanded reckoning of the world where right-side up must by extension have an upside down. To McMillian, the aesthetic process is closely related to the retelling of history, as the artist has the prerogative to build his or her own vision of reality, and the historian has wide leeway to choose what to emphasize and how to contextualize the story.

A more recent work, The Supreme Court Painting (2004), clearly embodies this ethos, rendering the solid doric proportions of the eponymous building

---

2. Holly Myers, "Disposable Society," Los Angeles Times, 13 October 2004, E6.

3. McMillian, conversation with the author.

in fluid swirls of blue and white acrylic. The giant canvas, cut to suggest the building's shape and left unstretched and drooping under the weight of its puddles of paint, pictorially seeks to turn marble into sky, but its ever-present materiality forestalls this conceit. The work taps into precedents found elsewhere in his production but breaks new ground by marrying a clear image to an ostensibly abstract gesture. Supreme Court's political message is also clear, as it questions how Greco-Roman architecture has come to represent present-day judicial ideals. While McMillian shows that historically favored aesthetic ideals are meant to inspire consensus, his brand of stylistic discord is intended to keep options (and minds) open.

WORKS IN THE EXHIBITION

UNTITLED, 2003
Oil on canvas
36 x 48 inches
Collection of Gaby and Wilhelm Schürmann,
Aachen, Germany

THE SUPREME COURT PAINTING, 2004
Poured acrylic on cut canvas
216 x 216 inches
Courtesy of the artist; Susanne Vielmetter
Los Angeles Projects; and Adamski Gallery
for Contemporary Art, Aachen, Germany

REPRESENTATION OF DESTABILIZATION
(RE: CF GAINES), 2005
Troughs
Dimensions variable
Courtesy of the artist; Susanne Vielmetter
Los Angeles Projects; and Adamski Gallery
for Contemporary Art, Aachen, Germany

UNTITLED, 2005
DVD
3 minutes, 41 seconds
Courtesy of the artist; Susanne Vielmetter
Los Angeles Projects; and Adamski Gallery
for Contemporary Art, Aachen, Germany

UNTITLED (LANDSCAPE), 2005
Charcoal and acrylic on canvas
96 x 360 inches
Courtesy of the artist; Susanne Vielmetter
Los Angeles Projects; and Adamski Gallery
for Contemporary Art, Aachen, Germany

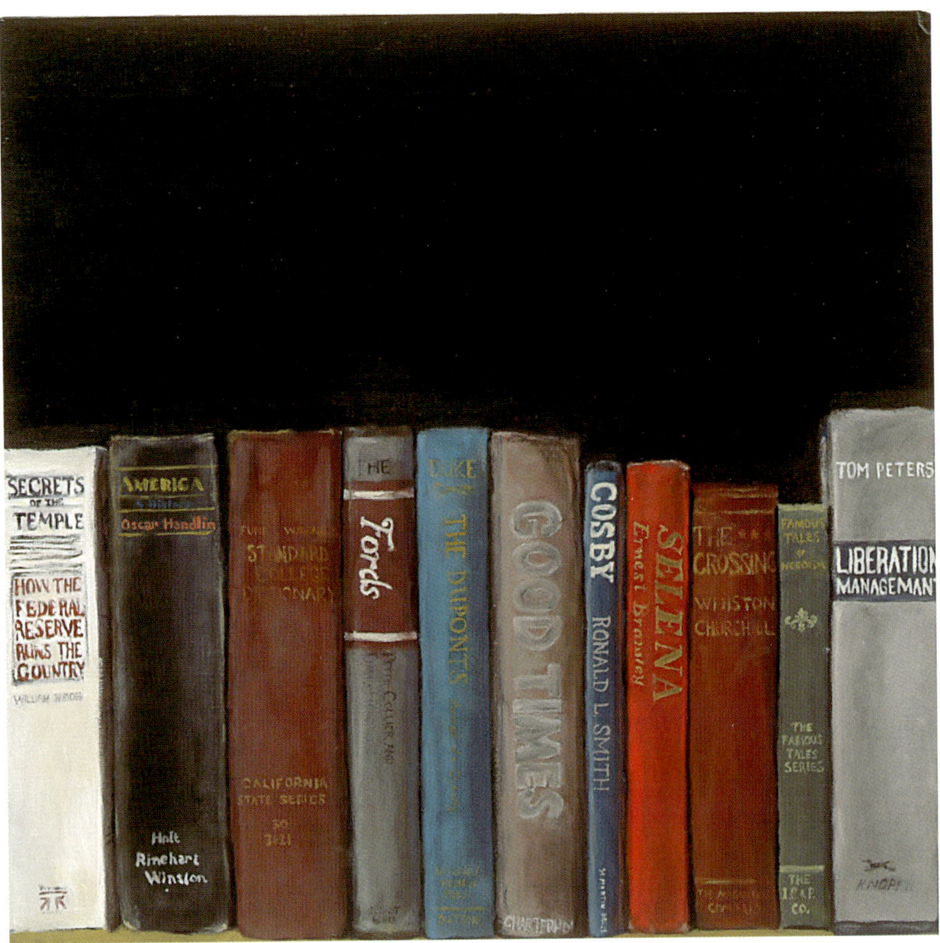

IN PROGRESS, 2003
Oil on wood
18 x 18 inches
Collection of Gaby and Wilhelm Schürmann, Aachen, Germany

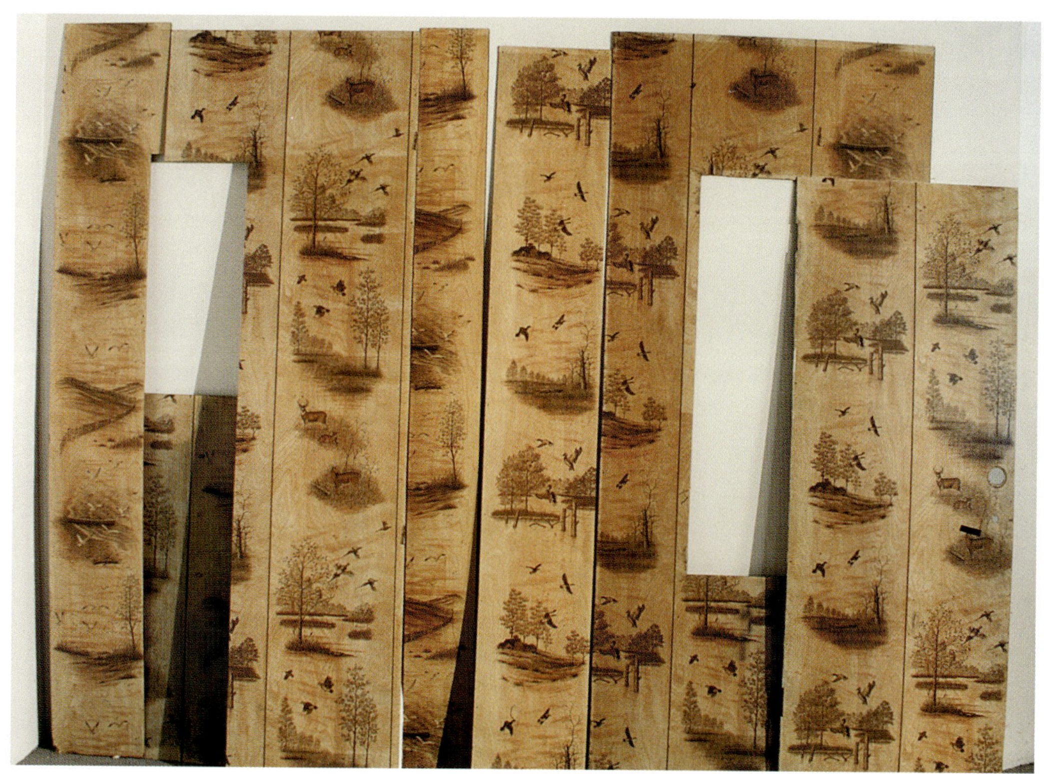

WOOD PANELING, 2004
Wood paneling
Dimensions variable
Collection of Eileen Harris Norton, Santa Monica

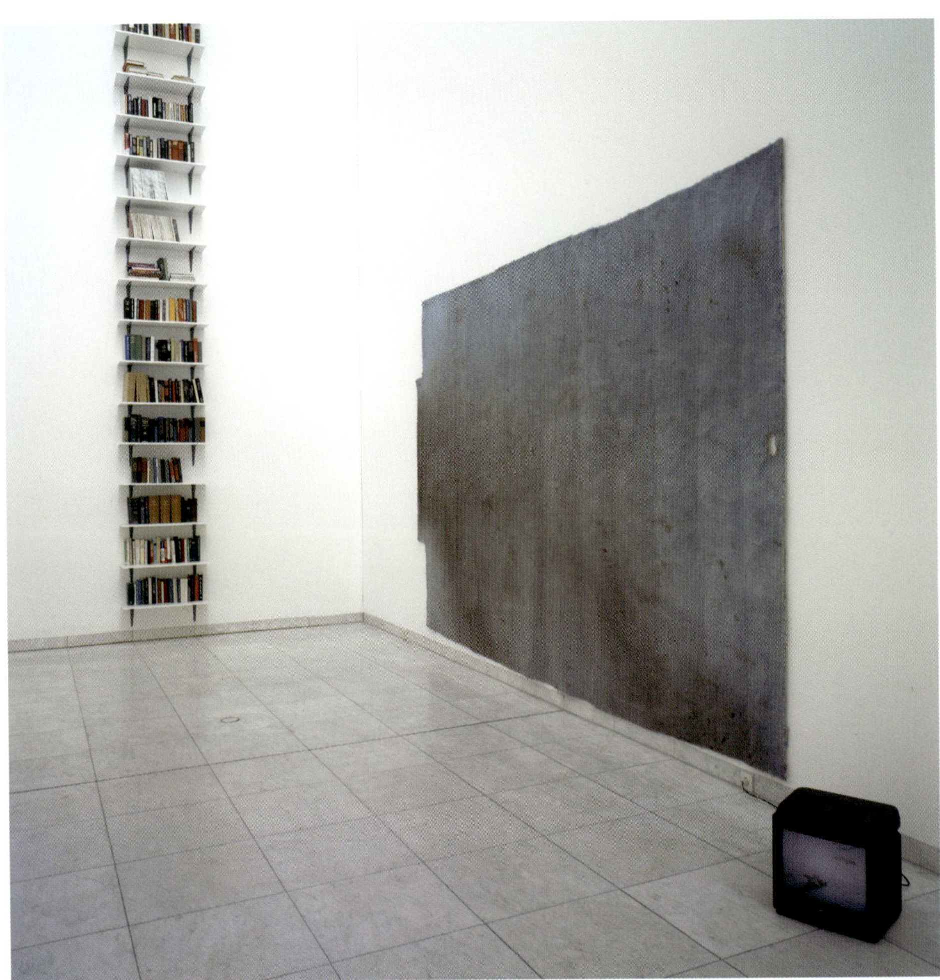

From left to right:
UNTITLED, 2005; UNTITLED, 2002; and THE DEATH OF A GRASSHOPPER (FOR L. TOLSTOY), 2005
"Menschengladbach," installation at Museum Abteiberg, Mönchengladbach, Germany, 2005

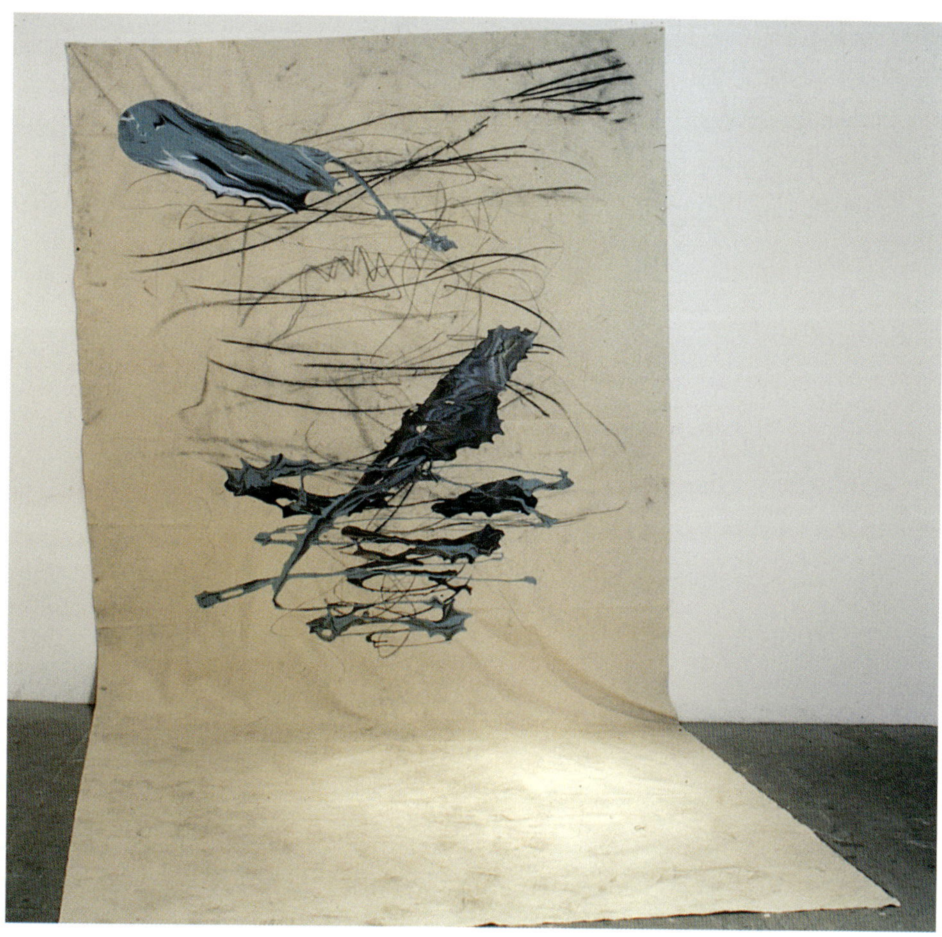

UNTITLED, 2004
Latex and charcoal on canvas
84 x 72 x 36 inches
Collection of Martin and Rebecca Eisenberg
Promised gift to the Studio Museum of Harlem, New York

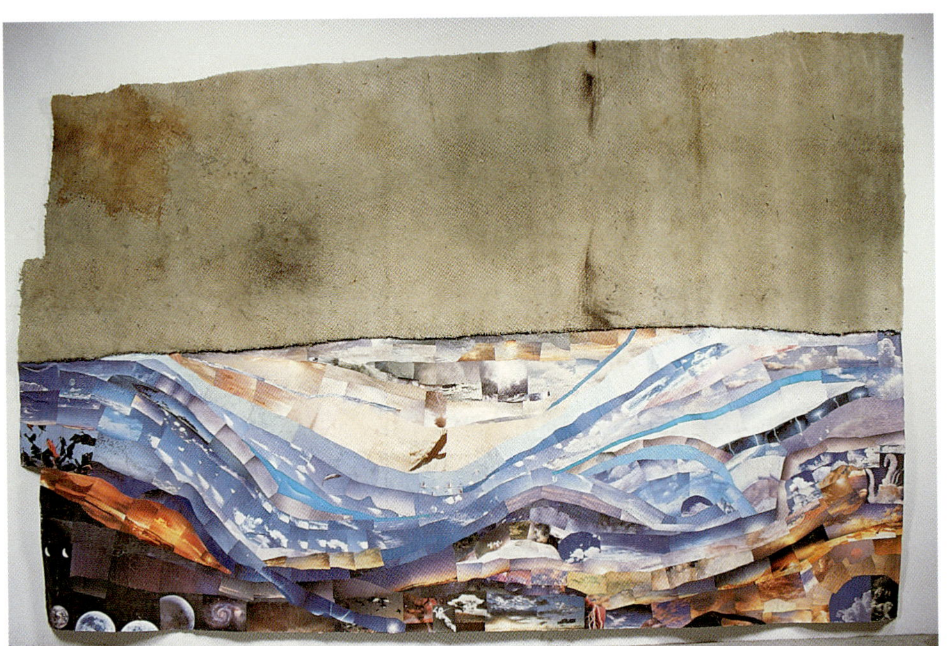

UNTITLED, 2003
Found carpet and paper on canvas
110 x 160 inches
Collection of Jeff Kerns, Los Angeles

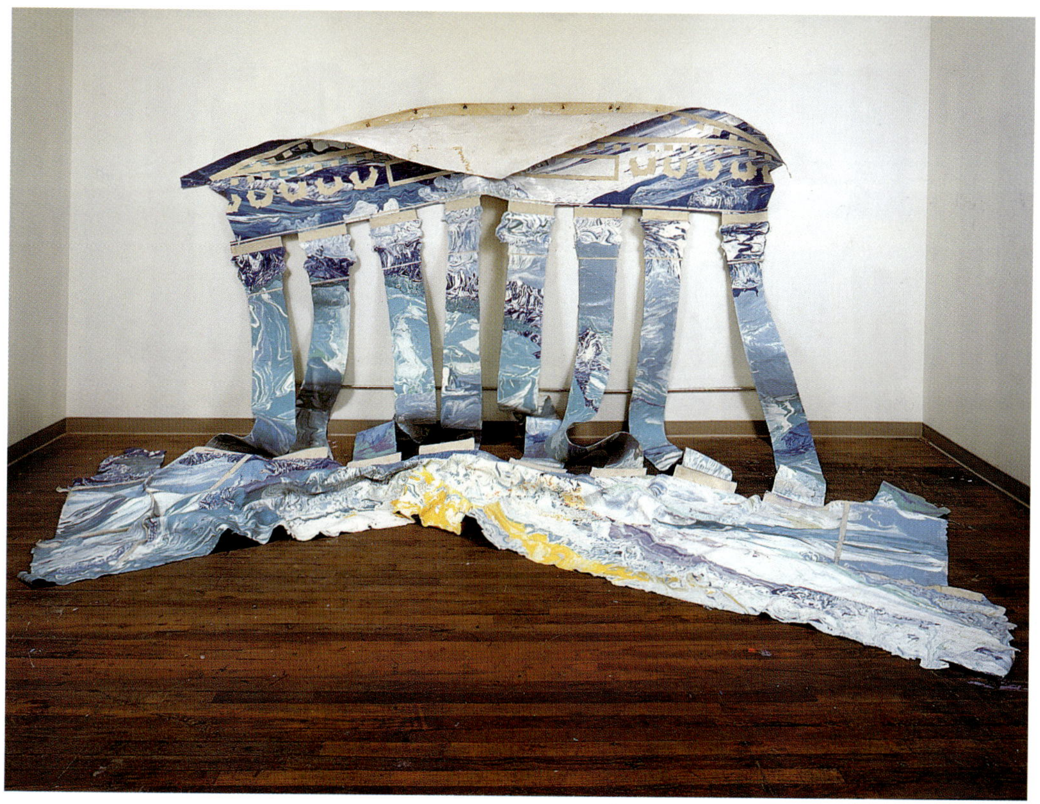

THE SUPREME COURT PAINTING, 2004
Poured acrylic paint on cut canvas
216 x 216 inches
Courtesy of the artist; Susanne Vielmetter Los Angeles Projects; and Adamski Gallery for
Contemporary Art, Aachen, Germany

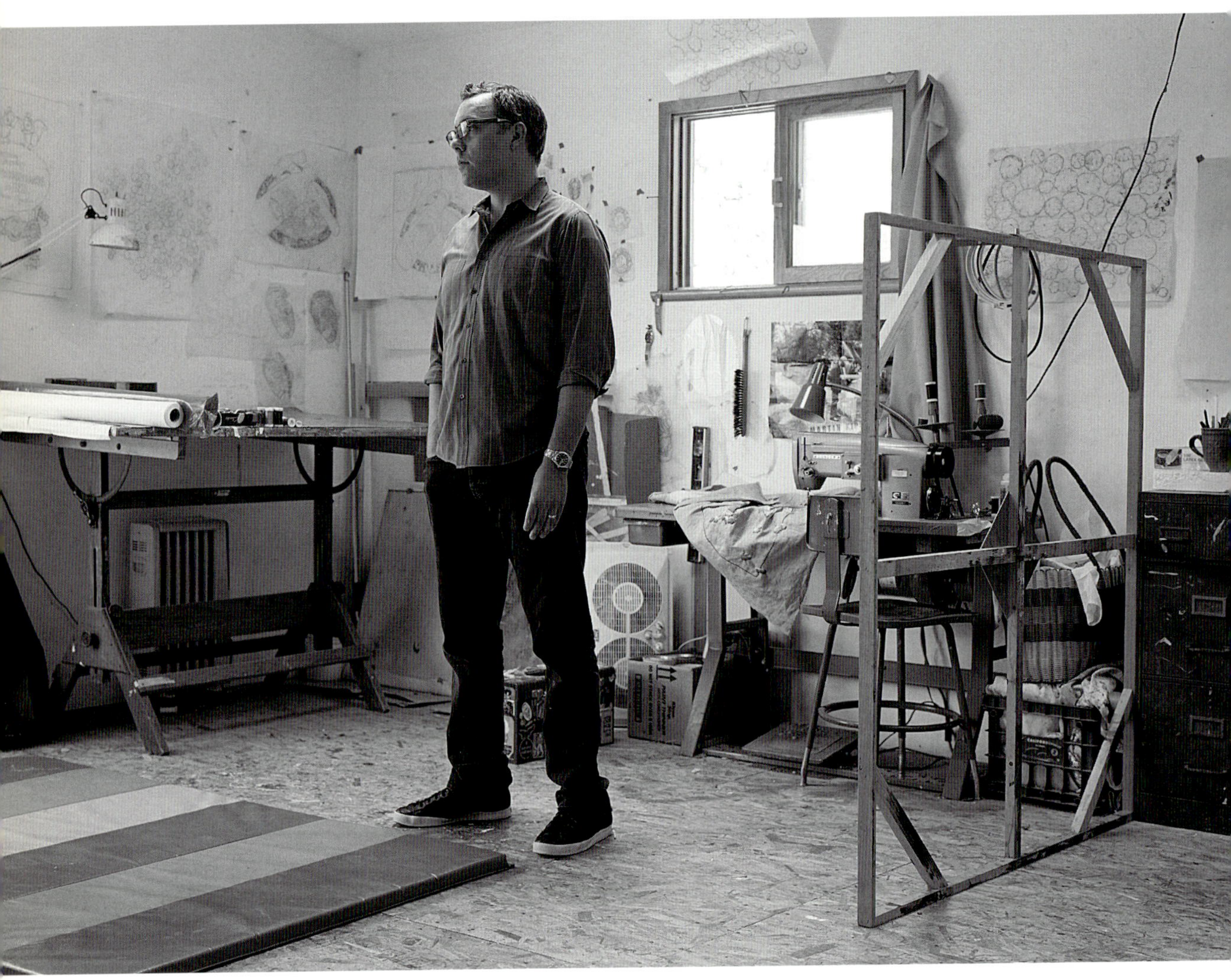

b. 1966, Burbank, California;
lives in Los Angeles

Selected Solo Exhibitions

2005 Patrick Painter Inc., Santa Monica,
     California
2004 Bernier/Eliades Gallery, Athens
2003 Patrick Painter Inc., Santa Monica,
     California
2002 Essor Gallery, London
2001 Frehrking Wiesehöfer, Cologne, Germany
     "Selections from 'A True Tale,'
     'Brazilian T-Shirt,' and 'Dig,'"
     Patrick Painter, Inc., Santa Monica,
     California
1998 George's, Los Angeles

Selected Group Exhibitions

2002 Galerie Ghislaine Hussenot, Paris
     "Startkapital," K21 Kunstsammlung
     Nordrhein-Westfalen, Düsseldorf, Germany
2000 "Paintland," Lemon Sky Project Space,
     Los Angeles

Selected Bibliography

- Boecker, Susanne von. "Explosive Geschichten
in Bildern: Ivan Morley in der Galerie
Frehrking Wiesehöfer." Kölner Stadt-Anzeiger
(Cologne, Germany), 8 November 2001, 18.
- Harvey, Doug. "Death-Stalking, Sleep-Walking,
Barbarian Ninja Terminators." L.A. Weekly
(2–8 March 2001): 39. Review of Patrick
Painter, Inc., exhibition.
- Kraus, Chris. "Ivan Morley at Frehrking
Wiesehöfer." Art in America 90, no. 6
(June 2002): 133.

Ivan Morley

Painting in Tongues

The vicissitudes of history and storytelling are at the heart of Ivan Morley's practice and have guided the development of his paintings over the past several years. Most often, the artist cobbles together a narrative text that purports to be based in historical fact but is admittedly clouded by memory. The bulk of these generative anecdotes address obscure wrinkles in the late-nineteenth- and early-twentieth-century development of California. For instance, the Dig series describes the archaeological discovery of what was said to be the largest red-light district ever excavated in California, and the True Tale series follows an entrepreneur who made a fortune shipping cats to San Francisco for vermin control. Morley works with these stories, picking up strands of information and attempting to give them visual form through an array of techniques. As each painting gets underway, however, its basis in a specific narrative loosens, often drifting into tangents and sometimes even blending with other stories. Morley defers the position of sole narrator to a chorus of observers, rendering the subject in ways that complicate the attribution of a single hand.

This can be seen in two identically titled and dated canvases, Tehachepi (sic) (2003), that pertain to a story about a high-desert town that experienced such strong gusts that bullets were always diverted to hit the windward side of its trees. In each of the differently sized paintings, a bullet-ridden tree is pictured but treated distinctly. In the larger one, stylized leaves are rendered with dense and variegated embroidery, and bullet holes are fashioned out of appliquéd florets of oil paint. The smaller canvas shows a similar but obviously different tree whose leaf clusters are rendered in a child-like fashion from flat patches of paint; gone are the didactic arrows indicating wind direction and bullet vectors found in the larger canvas. Morley originally exhibited these side by side, playing up their distinctions and explicitly demonstrating separate viewpoints of the same subject.

Morley's multiple perspective approach to his subject matter allows him to challenge his own predispositions towards painting and push himself into alternate or parallel traditions. He has experimented extensively with batik, for instance, as another way of integrating color and pattern on a fabric support, like oil on canvas. Distanced from the Romantic tradition of the authorial hand, batik's heritage is not only non-Western but kitschy and touristic (like the California "stoner" tradition in which Morley first encountered it).[1] Likewise, the artist has embraced painting on glass; first intrigued by its use as a cheap substitute for stained glass, Morley later appreciated its references to sign painting and tourist artifacts. (Ghanaian glass paintings made for the tourist trade first exposed him to this possibility.) In order to paint on glass, one must compose in reverse on the backside—painting in foreground first, then middle ground, then background—offering the perfect challenge for Morley's considerable skills and training. He has also used machine-stitched embroidery in place of the primary hand to provide a tangible record of time (one can literally count the threads to get a sense of how long a particular passage took to make). The tactility, level of sheen, saturation and range of color, and reaction with light of each of these techniques are chief considerations for how and when they are used.

One of the results (and aims) of Morley's method is to try to make objects that appear to be "souvenirs of a fictional as well as an actual place."[2] He strives for an "artifact quality" so that the works appear as if they have fallen out of time or indeed out of one of his chosen narratives.[3] His resistance to working in a dominant style contributes to this quality and allows the viewer to consider contexts and conditions outside the frame, including the work's informing narrative and the ingrained associations of the viewer, as well as the relationships between individual paintings. Morley has said that he is interested in tackling methods and subjects with a lot of "baggage" so that multiple associations and diverse histories are activated in the mind of the beholder.[4] Thus his use of California frontier-era imagery brings up rafts of preconceptions, just as painting on glass does. Certain motifs, such as the florets in Tehachepi (sic), morph and migrate from piece to piece and from narrative to narrative, problematizing the issue of meaning and drawing attention to the power of context.

81

1. Press release, Patrick Painter, Inc., Santa Monica, California, February 2003.

2. Press release, Essor Gallery, London, September 2002.

3. Ivan Morley, in conversation with the author, Los Angeles, 4 February 2005.

4. Ibid.

EL MONTE, 2001
Batik, oil, and thread on cotton
30 x 40 inches
Kourosh Larizadeh and Luis Pardo
Collection

EL MONTE, 2001
Batik, oil, and thread on cotton
36 x 48 inches
Collection of Gaby and Wilhelm Schürmann,
Aachen, Germany

AD, 2003
Oil on glass
24 x 20 inches
Collection of Wendy Chang and
Marcel Brichon, Vancouver

SAN GABRIEL, 2003
Oil on glass
36 x 30 inches
The Museum of Contemporary Art, Los Angeles
Purchased with funds provided by the
Curatorial Discretionary Fund

TEHACHEPI (SIC), 2003
Oil, acrylic, batik, thread, UV varnish,
and KY jelly on cotton
36 x 29 3/4 inches
Collection of Gaby and Wilhelm Schürmann,
Aachen, Germany

TEHACHEPI (SIC), 2003
Oil, batik, thread, and UV varnish
on cotton
41 x 33 inches
Collection of Gregory Papadimitriou, Athens,
Greece

LOGO, 2004
Oil, wax, and KY jelly on polyester over panel
24 x 25 inches
Collection of Sylvie Winckler, Brussels

EMBLEM, 2005
Acrylic and dye on leather over panel
44 x 25 1/2 inches
Kourosh Larizadeh and Luis Pardo
Collection

FROM DON, GEORGE, AND DIANE, 2005
Oil, wax, and KY jelly on canvas over panel
Approximately 78 x 66 inches
Courtesy of the artist and Patrick Painter,
Inc., Santa Monica

LOGO, 2005
Oil, acrylic dye, wax, KY jelly,
and UV varnish on linen over panel
43 1/4 x 36 1/8 inches
Kourosh Larizadeh and Luis Pardo
Collection

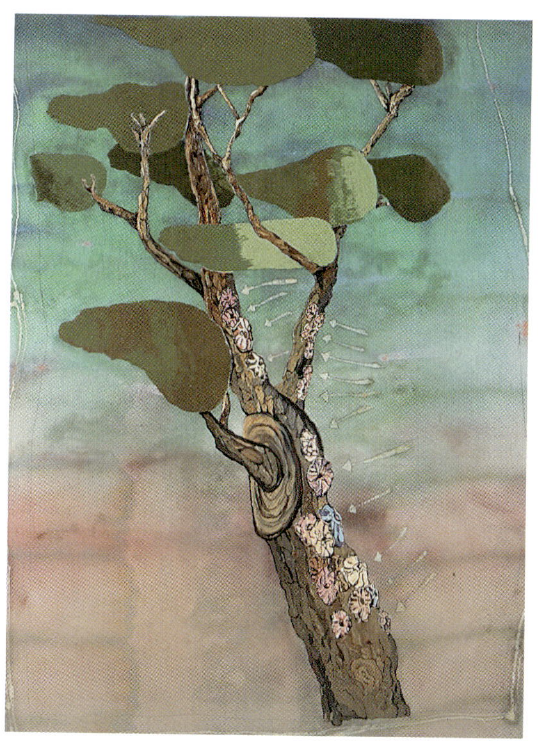

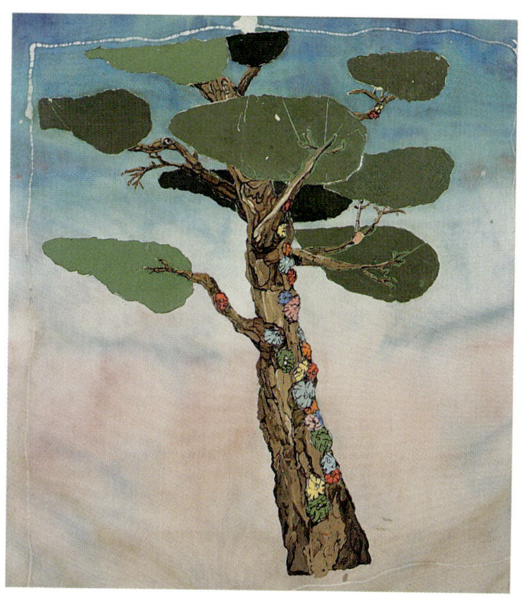

Top:
TEHACHEPI (SIC), 2003
Oil, acrylic, batik, thread, UV varnish,
and KY jelly on cotton
36 x 29 3/4 inches
Collection of Gaby and Wilhelm Schürmann,
Aachen, Germany

Bottom:
TEHACHEPI (SIC), 2002
Oil, batik, and UV varnish on canvas
31 x 28 inches
Collection of Mary Yoder, California

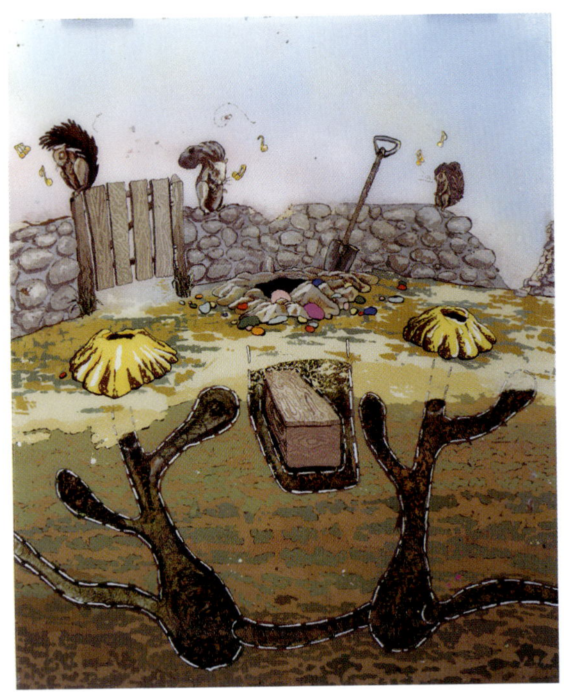

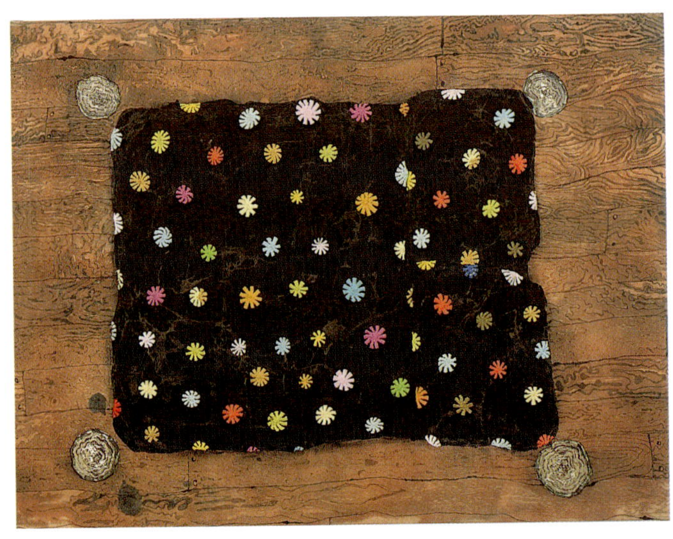

Top:
SAN GABRIEL, 2003
Oil on glass
36 x 30 inches
The Museum of Contemporary Art, Los Angeles
Purchased with funds provided by the
Curatorial Discretionary Fund

Bottom:
EL MONTE, 2001
Batik, oil, and thread on cotton
30 x 40 inches
Kourosh Larizadeh and Luis Pardo Collection

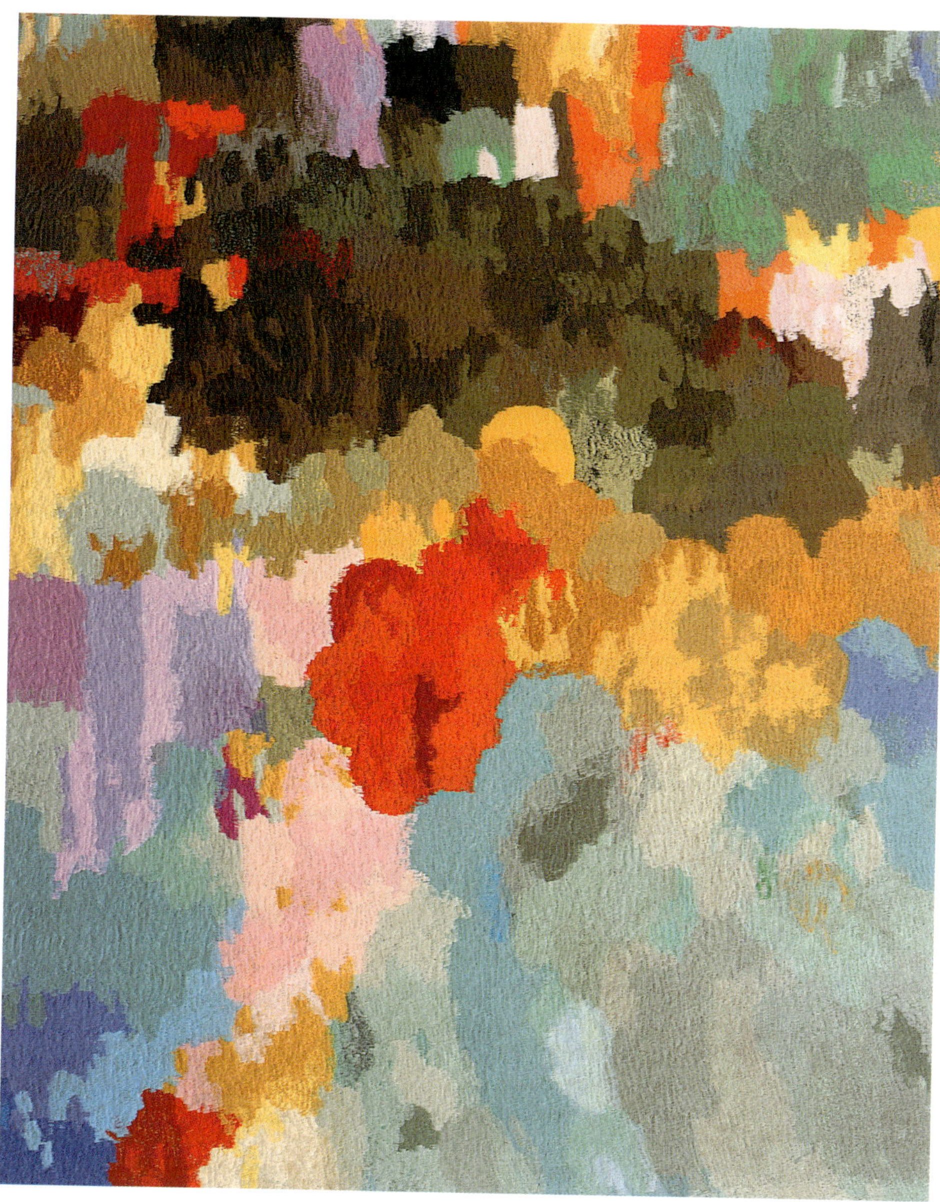

A TRUE TALE, 2005
Thread on canvas
53 x 43 inches
Collection of Thomas Dane, London

86

LOGO, 2005
Oil, acrylic dye, wax, KY jelly, and UV varnish on linen over panel
43 1/4 x 36 1/8 inches
Kourosh Larizadeh and Luis Pardo Collection

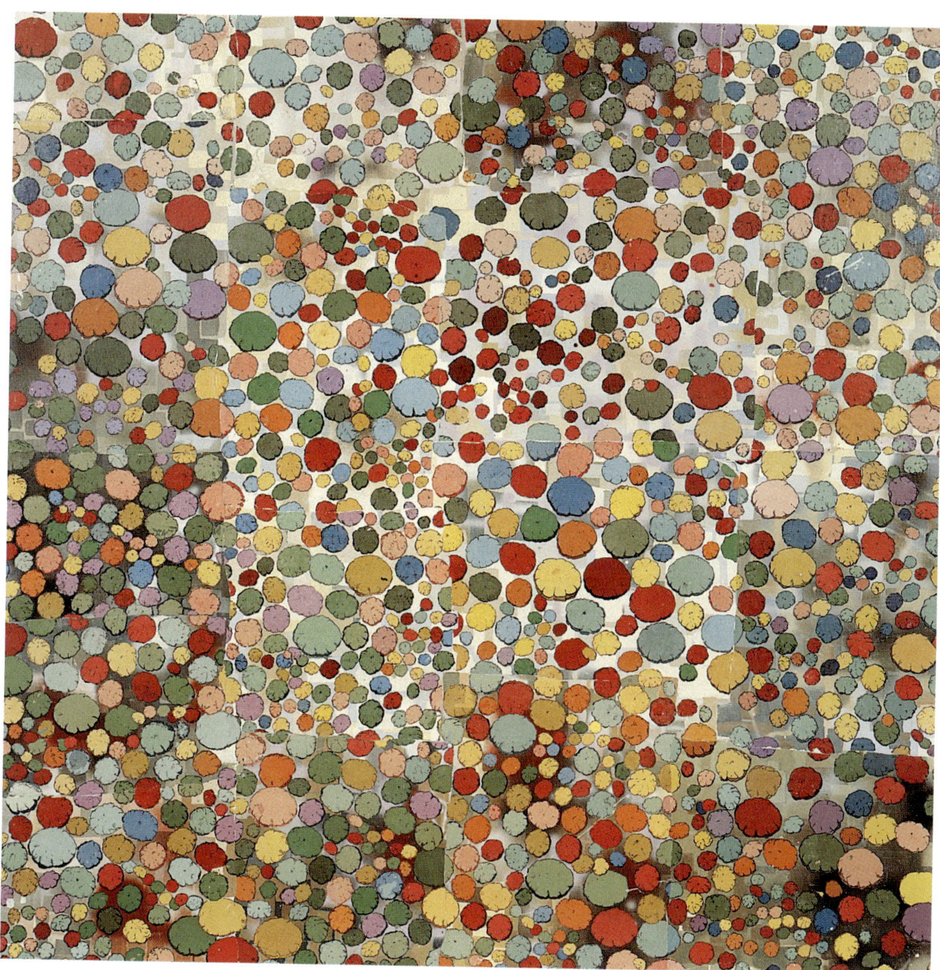

FROM DON, GEORGE, AND DIANE, 2005
Oil, wax, and KY jelly on polyester over panel
80 x 79 3/16 inches
Courtesy of Elizabeth Dee Gallery, New York

Anselm Reyle in his studio, Berlin, 2005
Aurelia Sellin, ANSELM REYLE (from the Dans l'atelier series), 2005, photograph,
38 3/16 x 27 15/16 inches, private collection

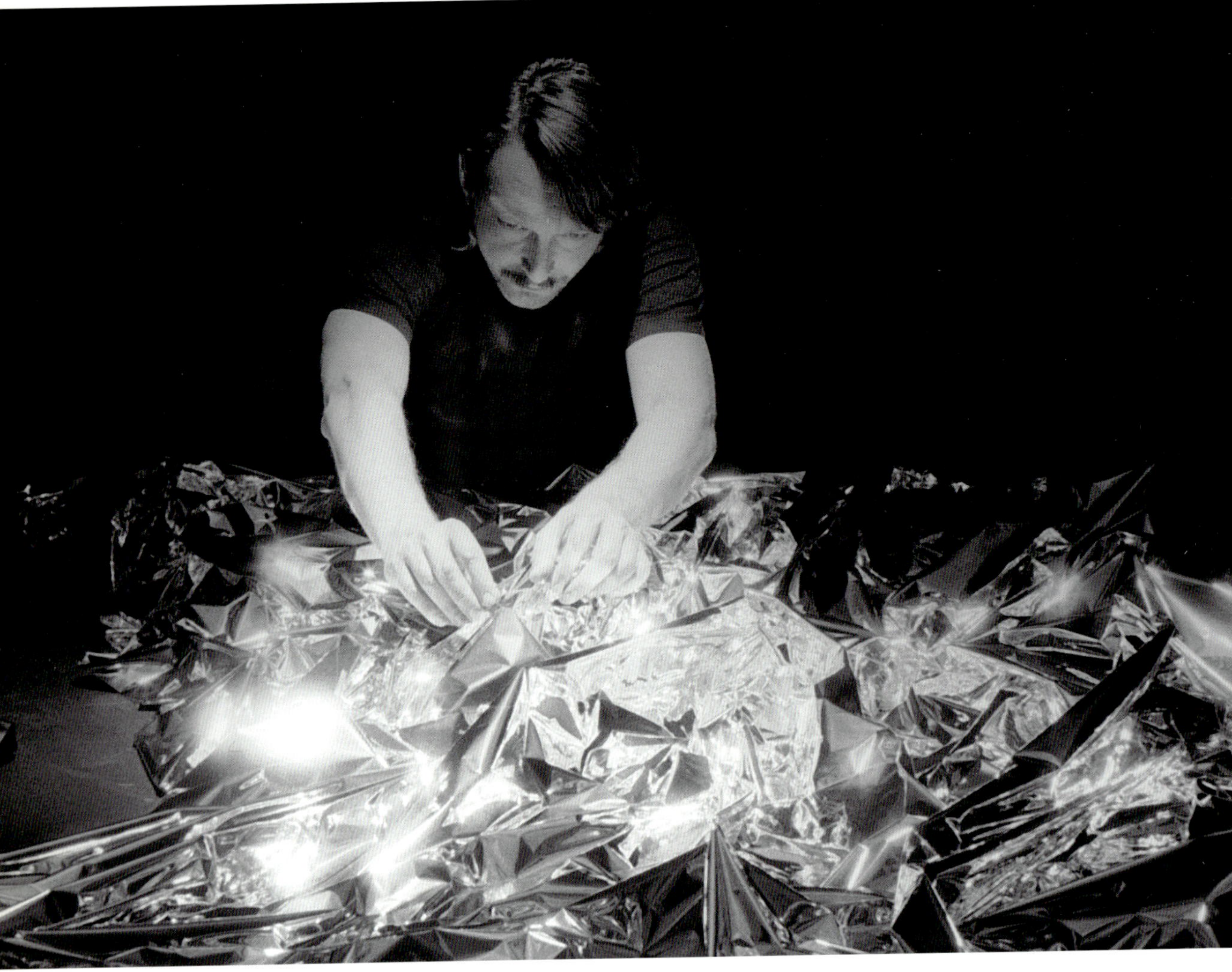

b. 1970, Tübingen, Germany;
lives in Berlin

Selected Solo Exhibitions

2006 "Mexican Mushrooms," kurimanzutto,
     Mexico City
2005 "Life Enigma," Galerie Giti Nourbakhsch,
     Berlin
2004 "Trilogy of Broken Light," The Modern
     Institute, Glasgow, Scotland
     "Farbe und Licht," Neuer Aachener Kunst-
     verein, Aachen, Germany
     "The Art of Anselm Reyle," Gavin Brown's
     Enterprise, New York
2002 "trust," Galerie Jennifer Flay, Paris
     "at the edge of forever," Roma Roma
     Roma, Rome
2001 "beyond," Galerie Giti Nourbakhsch,
     Berlin
2000 Galerie Giti Nourbakhsch, Berlin

Selected Group Exhibitions

2005 "Expanded Painting," Prague Bienniale 2,
     Prague
     "Sculptures d'appartement," Musée
     Départemental d'Art Contemporain,
     Rochechouart, France
     Galerie Almine Rech, Paris
2004 "Formalismus: Moderne Kunst, Heute,"
     Kunstverein, Hamburg, Germany
     "Malerei," Galerie Rüdiger Schöttle,
     Munich, Germany
     "It's All an Illusion," Migros Museum
     für Gegenwartskunst, Zürich, Switzerland
2003 "Definitively Provisional," Whitechapel
     Project Space, London
     "Deutschemalereizweitausenddrei," Kunst-
     verein, Frankfurt, Germany (exh. cat.)

Anselm Reyle

2002 "My head is on fire but my heart is
     full of love," Charlottenborg
     Udstillingsbygning, Copenhagen
     (exh. cat.)
     "Schwartzwaldhochstrasse: Aktuelle
     Kunst in und aus Baden-Württemberg,"
     Staatliche Kunsthalle, Baden-Baden,
     Germany
2001 "Viva November," Kunstverein,
     Wolfsburg, Germany
     "Circles 5: Montana Sacra," Zentrum für
     Kunst und Medientechnologie, Karlsruhe,
     Germany

Selected Bibliography

- Anselm Reyle. Exh. cat. Berlin: Galerie
Giti Nourbakhsch; New York: Gavin Brown's
Enterprise; and Glasgow, Scotland: The Modern
Institute, 2004.
- Bell, Kirsty. "The Salvage City." Art Review
2, no. 7 (July–August 2004): 62–67.
- ———. "Anselm Reyle." Frieze, no. 86
(October 2004): 153.

Anselm Reyle has committed himself to examining the possibilities of abstraction, finding such a defined field to be anything but limiting. He has cast his net extremely wide, gathering up as many modes for making abstract pictures as possible while thinking about how to make them fresh, relevant, and contemporary. Each work evokes art-historical precedents and the value judgments they carry, but these works do not settle easily into pre-established categories, as they typically undergo modification in his studio. Often, humbly scaled precedents are super-sized to pump up their effects, hot day-glo colors and shiny mylar are applied to break with tradition, and optical distortions allow familiar styles to be seen in new ways.

Reyle's exhibitions push his manipulations of recognizable abstract genres even further, often through jarring juxtapositions that flaunt the distinctions between pieces. His 2004 exhibition at the Neuer Aachener Kunstverein in Aachen, Germany, was chock-full of contradictions—placing brushy pastel monochromes next to neon yellow ones, skewed interpretations of Victor Vasarely next to shiny silver-on-black canvases—while other works sported drips, stripes, and various motifs for organizing color across fields. His 2005 show "Life Enigma" at Galerie Giti Nourbakhsch in Berlin likewise combined various sorts of abstractions, ranging from paintings to ceiling-suspended assemblages of discarded neon sign material to freestanding pedestal-bound sculptures derived from cheap African tourist objects. The equivalency accorded to all of these untitled works from 2005 within the space emphatically served notice that the entire field of nonobjective art is at Reyle's disposal, and he aims to use it any way he likes. The green untitled painting (2005) from the "Life Enigma" exhibition is from a series that has been particularly fecund within Reyle's practice and relies on the unpredictability of mylar to create different patterns and effects. In addition to those with black grounds and silver figures, Reyle combined colored mylar with matching or contrasting background colors, sometime even adding spatters of gravity-defying paint. The shrill materials and hues, along with their often large scale, marks a radical shift from any high-art precedents these works may have—particularly the soft white Achromes of Piero Manzoni or the furrowed burlap of Alberto Burri—drawing them closer to low art. For example, the stark contrasts and high-sheen metallics, not to mention their protective Plexi boxes, vaguely hint at slick 1970s decorative schemes. Reyle welcomes such aesthetic impurity and has said that he is perhaps even more interested in subcultural uses of abstraction.[1]

This interest has perhaps most explicitly played itself out in Reyle's pairings of glazed ceramic objects and paintings. In the past, he has placed found vases and other vessels in close proximity to abstract canvases on the wall to provoke an often-jarring dialogue. In Lampe (2005), he takes this activity one step further, integrating an abstract drip painting of his own making with the shade of a 1960s-era brown ceramic lamp. Through this simple gesture, the painting is implicated into a complicated system that extends from avant-garde to rear guard, where the high-minded aspirations of early twentieth-century abstractionists find themselves reduced over time to decorator backdrops. Reyle makes it difficult to assess where in that scheme this object belongs and, in so doing, forces a broader consideration of how abstract imagery has infiltrated our culture.

Reyle has pushed other non-art objects into the purview of his public as well, selecting anachronistic items such as antique butter churns, hay wagons, field plows, and spinning wheels and subjecting them to manipulations ranging from the subtle to the garish. Wagenrad (2003) is one such work, in which a blue neon light affixed to the back of a wood wagon wheel pushes a piece of kitschy interior décor to a new level. As one can see here, his interventions usually consist of adding non-native color and end up high-lighting the inherent graphic or structural beauty of the objects. The found sculptures are yet another device for disrupting any straightforward readings of his paintings, serving as mundane temporal or technological markers that allow the viewer to recognize the difference between present and past.

The world of found objects seems inexhaustible, just as Reyle's stripe paintings offer an exponential number of compositional combinations. This series asserts itself on the environment through harsh color combinations, errant drips, and reflective mylar or mir-rored Plexi insertions. In some, such as Untitled (2005), automotive lacquer is used and

1. Anselm Reyle, in conversation with the author, Berlin, 18 October 2004.

the density of the color is not stable—some stripes are even applied using cloud-painting techniques borrowed from Do-It-Yourself TV artiste Bob Ross. These works do not disturb for disturbance's sake, however, and their intensity and hue, flatness and sheen, are carefully calibrated so that the eye dances excitedly from edge to edge. Together with the rest of his ever-expanding repertoire, they form a collection of open systems that lead outward in every direction, ensuring that Reyle, like the other artists in "Painting in Tongues," has a virtually unencumbered palette of options to explore.

WORKS IN THE EXHIBITION

UNTITLED, 2005
Mixed media on canvas
117 x 55 inches
Courtesy of the artist, Berlin; Galerie Giti
Nourbakhsch, Berlin; and GBE Modern, New York

UNTITLED, 2005
Mixed media on canvas
117 x 55 inches
Courtesy of the artist, Berlin; Galerie Giti
Nourbakhsch, Berlin; and GBE Modern, New York

UNTITLED, 2005
Mixed media on canvas
117 x 55 inches
Courtesy of the artist, Berlin; Galerie Giti
Nourbakhsch, Berlin; and GBE Modern, New York

UNTITLED, 2005
Mixed media on canvas
117 x 55 inches
Courtesy of the artist, Berlin; Galerie Giti
Nourbakhsch, Berlin; and GBE Modern, New York

UNTITLED, 2005
Mixed media on canvas with acrylic glass
92 x 78 3/8 x 7 7/8 inches
Collection of Rena Conti and Ivan Moskowitz,
Brookline, Massachusetts

UNTITLED, 2005
Bronze, chrome, varnish, and makessa veneer
35 1/16 x 18 1/8 x 15 3/8 inches; plinth:
27 1/2 x 19 3/4 x 19 3/4 inches
Collection of Rena Conti and Ivan Moskowitz,
Brookline, Massachusetts

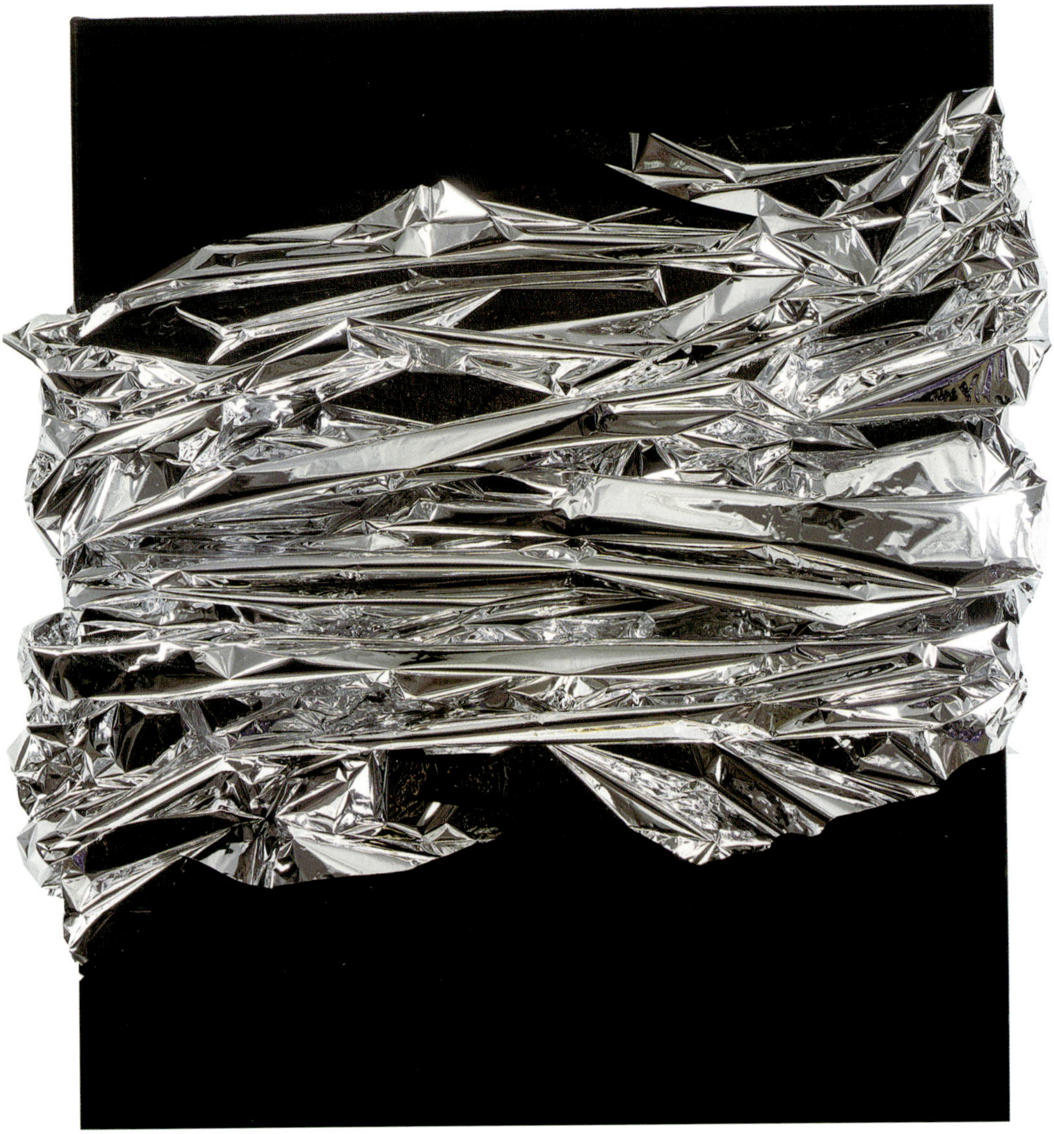

UNTITLED, 2005
Mixed media on canvas behind acrylic box
26 3/8 x 22 1/16 x 2 3/4 inches
Courtesy Andersen-S Contemporary Art, Copenhagen

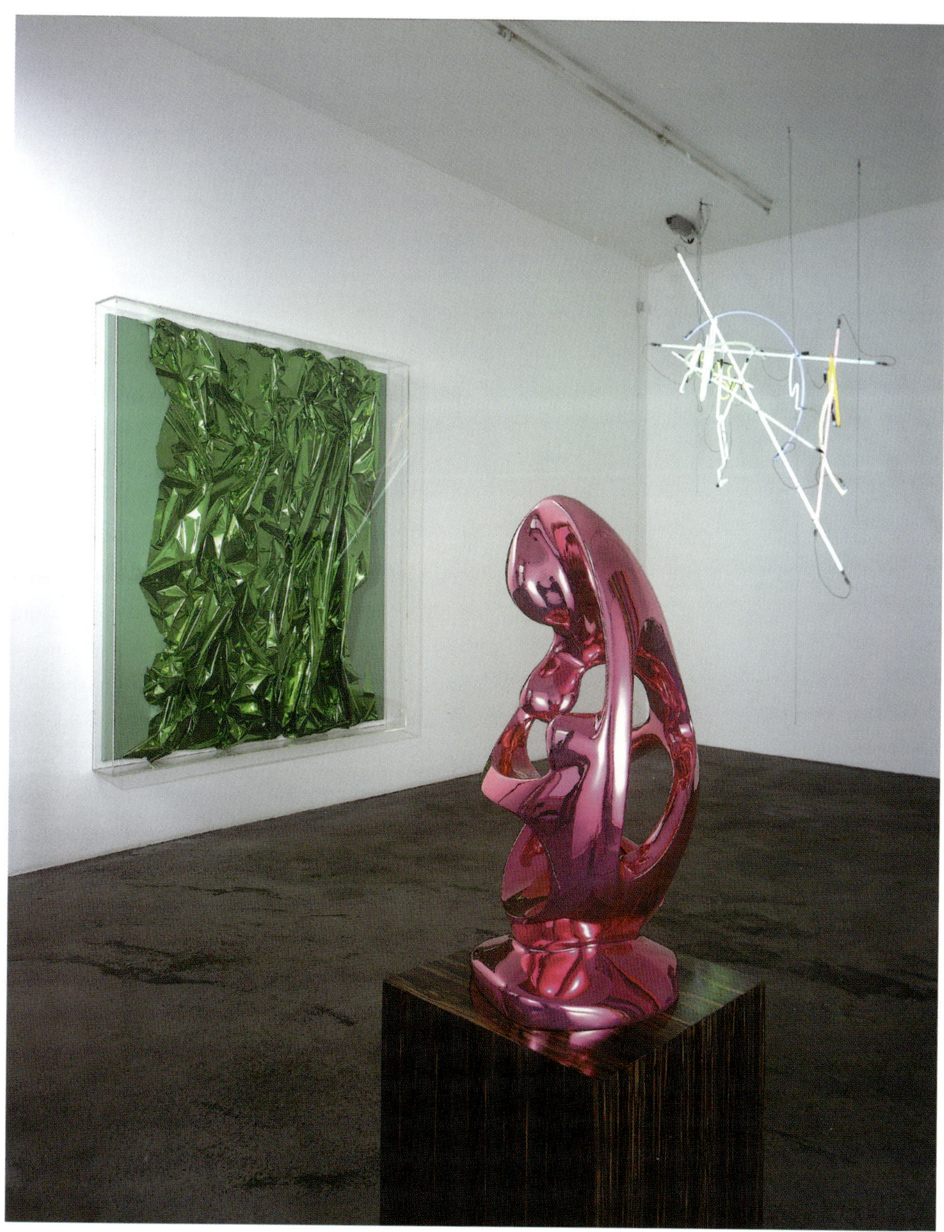

"Life Enigma," installation at Galerie Giti Nourbakhsch, Berlin, 2005

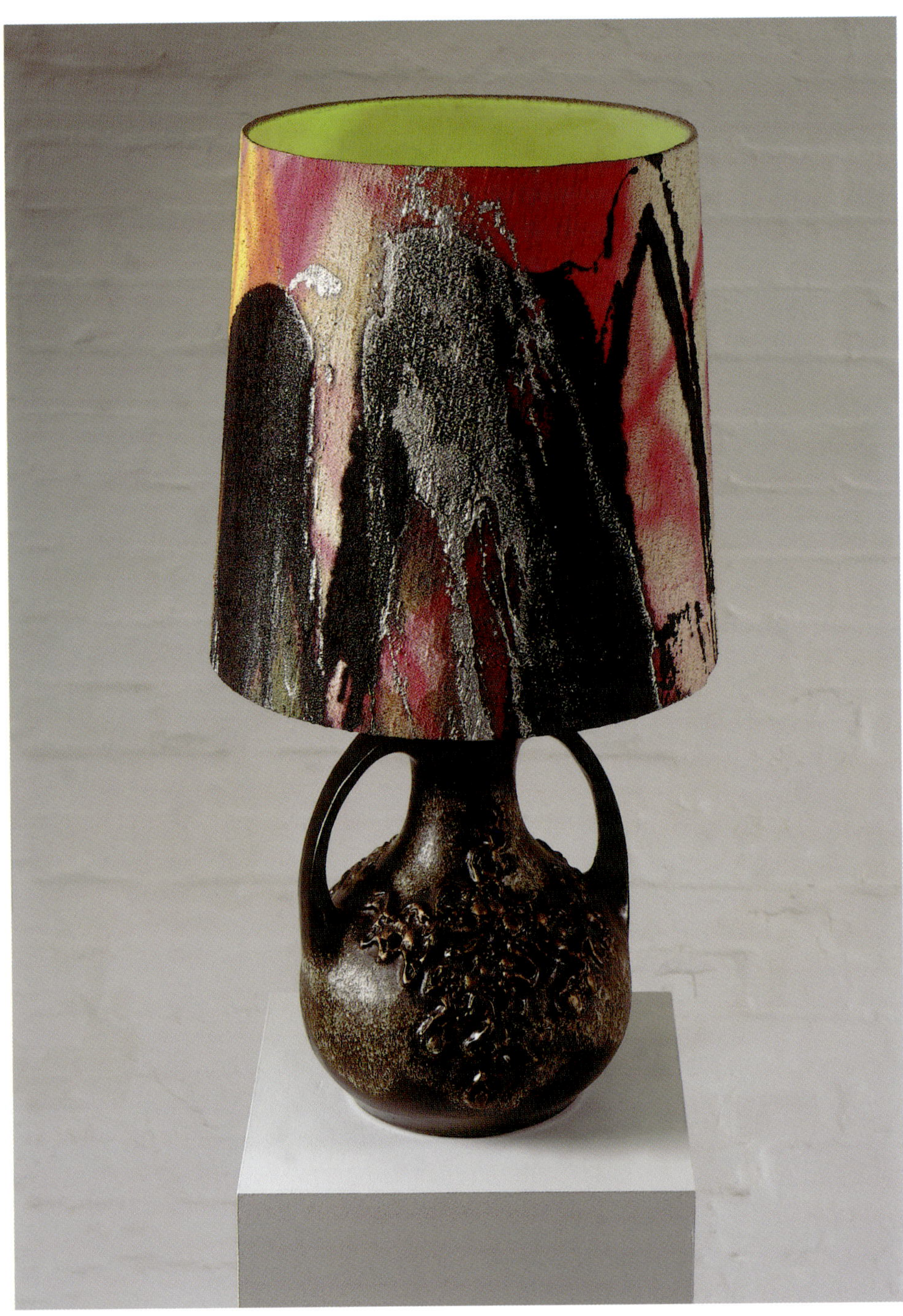

96

LAMPE, 2005
Mixed media on found object and light
31 1/2 x 17 5/16 x 17 5/16 inches
Courtesy Galerie Giti Nourbakhsch, Berlin

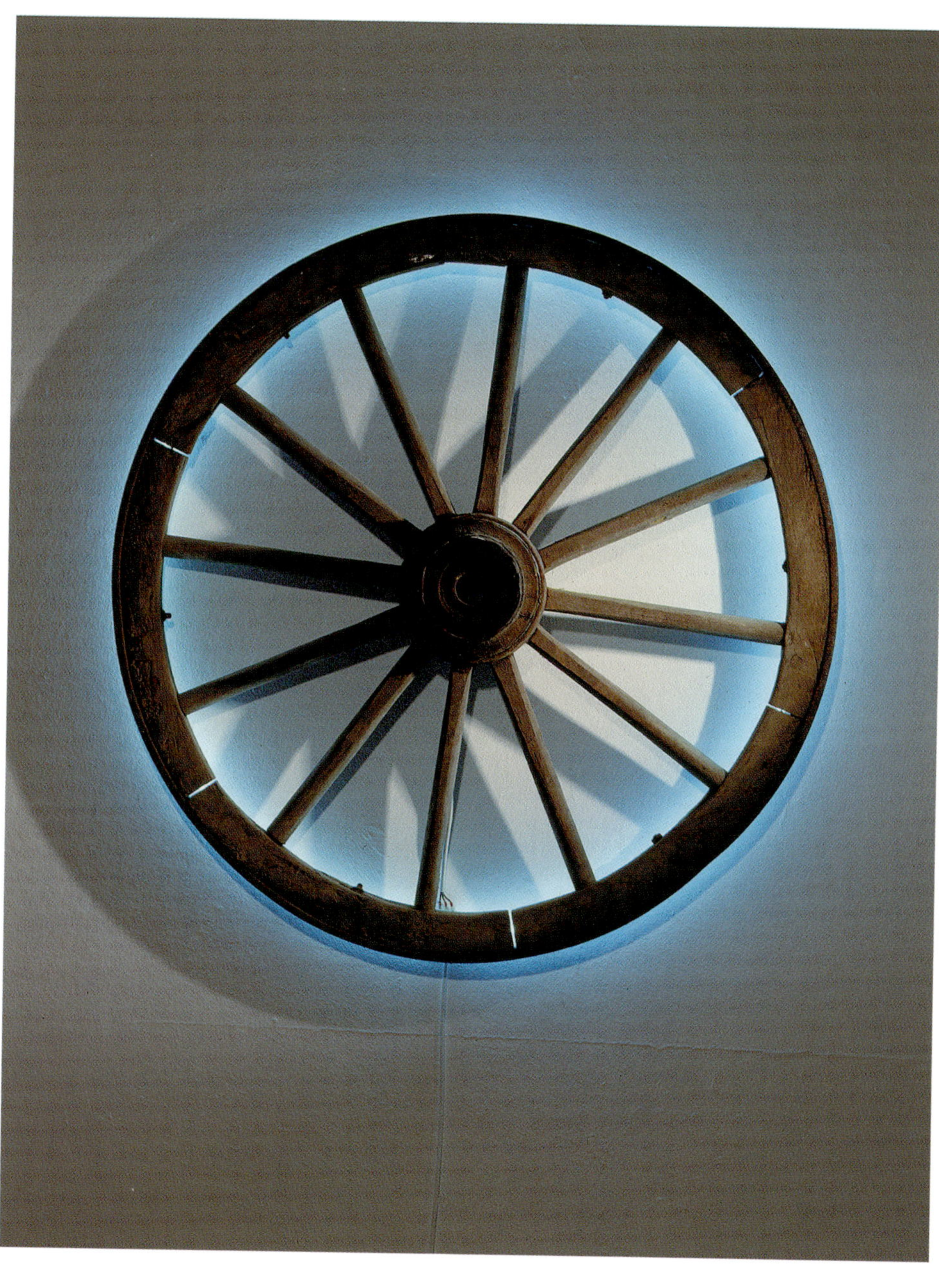

, 2003
Found object and neon
Diameter: 31 1/2 inches
Private collection, Berlin

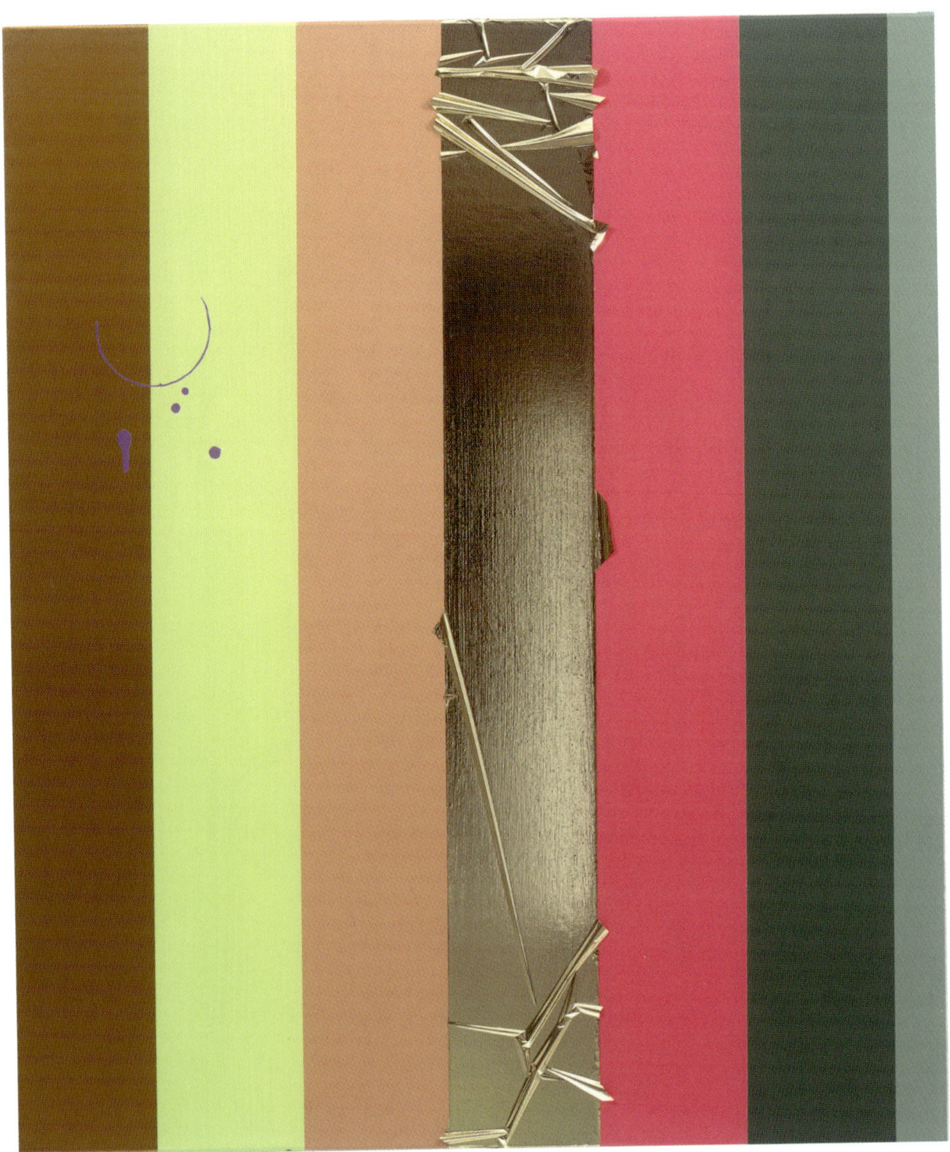

UNTITLED, 2005
Mixed media on canvas
53 1/8 x 44 7/8 inches
Private collection, Germany

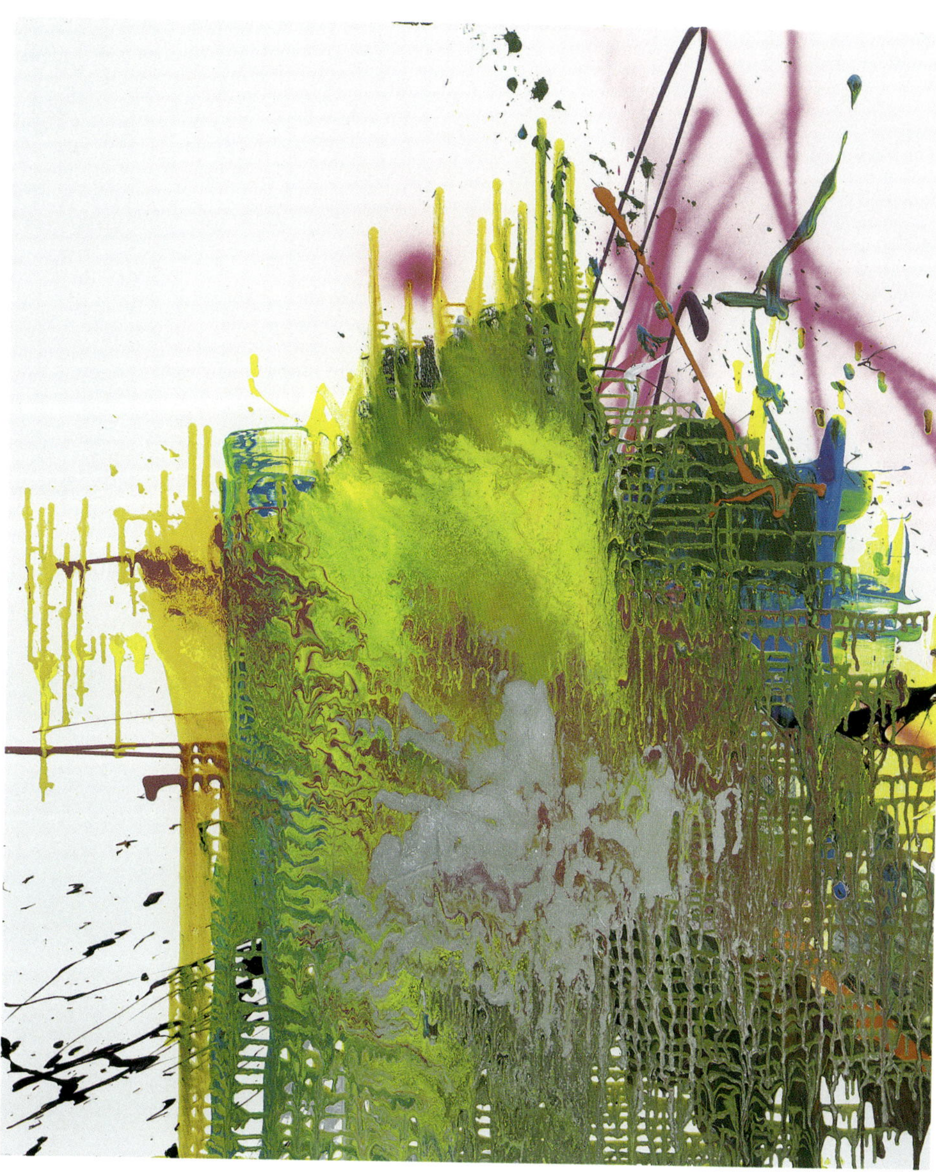

UNTITLED, 2004
Mixed media on canvas
53 1/8 x 44 7/8 inches
Private collection, New York

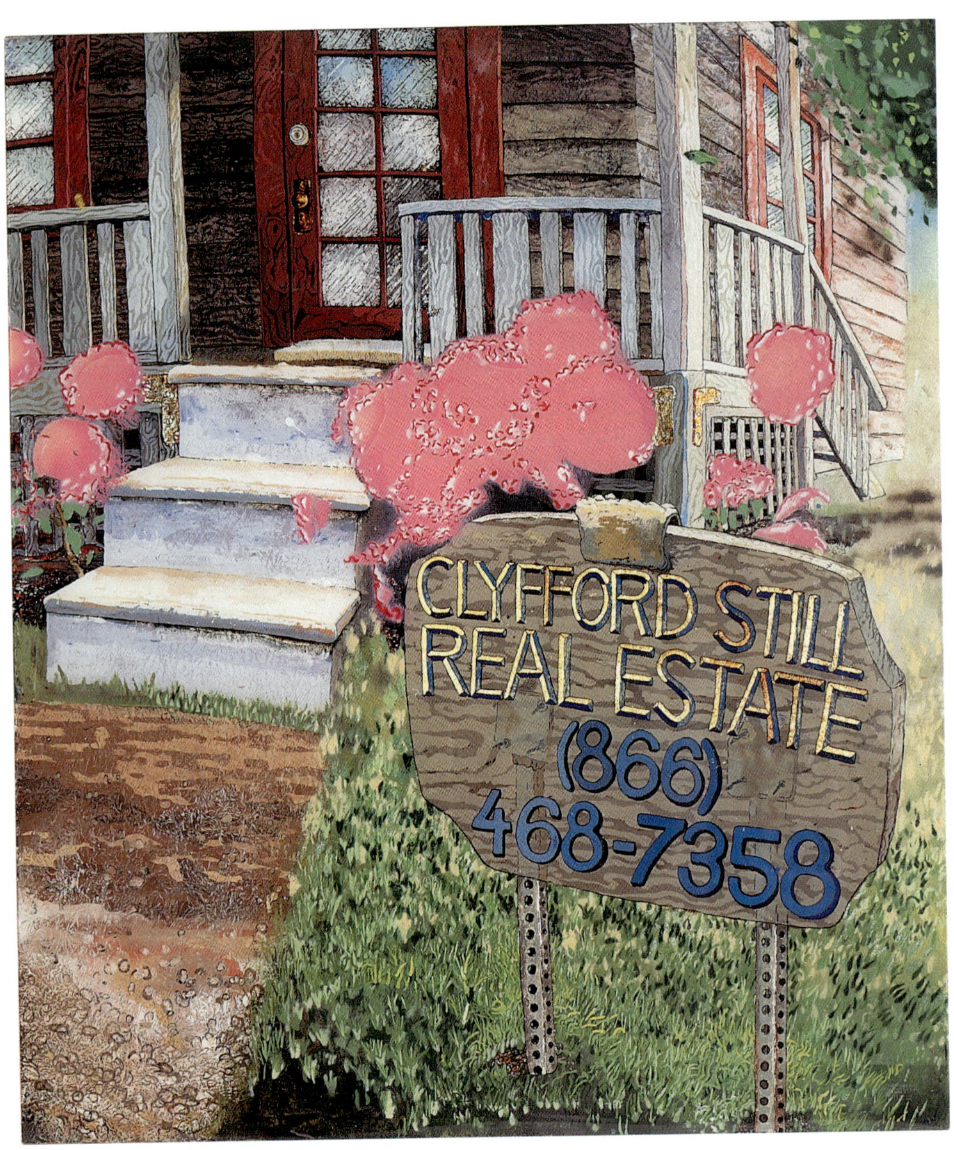

Ivan Morley
FROM DON, GEORGE, AND DIANE, 2003
Oil and gold and aluminum leaf on glass
36 x 31 inches
Collection of Heiner Bastian, Germany

"PAINTING IN TONGUES": REFLECTIONS ON A TITLE, AND AT THE VERY END
A QUESTION ABOUT THE ART THAT TITLE IS GIVEN TO

Friedrich Wolfram Heubach

It may or may not be the case that the title of this exhibition, "Painting
in Tongues," accurately describes the exhibited artists' intentions for
their work and their conceptions of themselves. However, it cannot be
disputed that the title points to a feeling of irritation that virtually
every visitor will experience when confronted with these artists' works.
With their numerous allusions to antecedent artistic or non-artistic
pictorial forms, these works run fundamentally counter to certain widespread views of the avant-garde and artistic progress—views that, in
the context of self-congratulatory modernism, often go so far as the
a priori claim that, when an artist of today makes use of anything an
earlier artist made history with, his work cannot possibly have anything
new and independent to offer but merely reveals his lack of originality,
reveals that he himself is a phenomenon of yesterday.

Not only, however, do the artists in "Painting in Tongues" make it
a veritable practice to turn to pre-existing pictorial worlds in their
works, some of them employ a variability of subjects, materials, and
styles that can be unsettling. After all, it makes it difficult, if not

impossible, for the viewer to recognize in their works that unmistakable
and wholly personal signature that has been regarded since time immemorial
as the badge of every higher—indeed, of all true—artistry. And hence
one may easily come to feel that something is missing, something the
artist would be especially determined to produce (and something everyone
is so concerned about): authenticity. That is, that "being-with-itself"
of the subject in all its actions, that unity of person which, as
"identity," the whole world constantly proclaims to be an indispensable
condition of human existence.

It would therefore not be at all surprising if a visitor to this exhibition—already dogged by the reservation "What is in any way authentic
about this art?!," and who yet again tries to determine if the work really
comes from the artist and time that it seems to—should finally lose pa-
tience and ask himself, "Who or what is actually manifesting itself in
these works? Who is speaking here?" And with this, the question broached
is one that the world has long faced when confronted with the curious
phenomenon suggested by this exhibition's title: "speaking in tongues."

Is it possible that a certain degree of insight into this phenomenon—
an excursus on the history and concept of "speaking in tongues"—might
make the "painting in tongues" that this exhibition highlights more
accessible to its irritated visitor? That it might even offer an answer
to the question, "Who is it that is speaking here, painting here?"

EXCURSUS

"Speaking in tongues"—the technical term is "glossolalia"—refers to
a form of speech that is not guided by the speaker's conscious will either
with respect to its content or its physical production. The speaker's
tongue articulates sounds without his conscious control, and the resulting

utterances range from mere stammering ("the blurting out of sounds that bear a formal resemblance to words or mere syllables"), to language-like productions ("speech in what seem to be distorted or fantastical languages"), to productions that are in every way identical with linguistic ones ("speech in the speaker's native language or a foreign language or dialect").[1]

Glossolalia is primarily discussed in the context of the history of religion as a marginal phenomenon in pagan religions, but which had a certain importance in ancient Greek religious practice and the ecstatic mysticism of Hellenism (particularly in the Delphic Pythia's pronouncements) and then played a very central role in early Christianity. In the Christian context, speaking in tongues—described in the New Testament as speech "in new languages" (Mark 16:17) or "in foreign languages" (Acts 10:46, 19:6)—was originally connected with the events that took place among Jesus's followers during Pentecost (Acts 2), when "they were all filled with the Holy Spirit and began to speak in other tongues, as the Spirit gave them utterance" (Acts 2:4). The early Christians regarded this phenomenon as an instance of speech inspired by the Holy Spirit, and they viewed it as one of those special spiritual gifts they called charismata. Today, by contrast, it is primarily the followers of the so-called Pentecostal movement who continue to hold the phenomenon in high esteem and incorporate it into religious practice.

A remarkable feature of speaking in tongues as it was understood at the time (for example by Paul, who practiced it himself)—and one that may come as a welcome consolation to this "multilingual" exhibition's bewildered visitor—is that it was only considered to be edifying for the speaker himself, while being of no benefit to any others present, including the speaker's own understanding (1 Corinthians 14:14 and 16).

1. See Hans Rust, *Das Zungenreden: Eine Studie zur kritischen Religionspsychologie* (Munich, Germany: J. F. Bergmann, 1924).

In this sense, the phenomenon of speaking in tongues—in the words of
a theological lexicon—is only "a miracle of speech and not one of hearing."
Like other phenomena of religious life, speaking in tongues tends to be
viewed by the sciences today from a clinical or psychopathological perspective. It is often described as a hypnotic or hysterical symptom, as auto-
matism. Most commonly, however, it is regarded as a symptom of schizophrenia,[2]
assimilated to the symptoms of dysphasia, and interpreted, for example,
as the "attempt to express the new and unprecedented quality of patho-
logical experiences with words and phrases that, similarly, have never
been heard before...and which completely replace the conventional words."[3]

Brief as this excursus is, it does provide an answer to the question
of who is actually speaking when the "tongues speak." While the answer
is not a simple one, it is nonetheless quite clear: if not the Holy
Spirit, then sheer insanity. It is not this answer alone that makes one
reluctant to draw conclusions of any kind about what this exhibition
presents as "painting in tongues" from what was said above about "speaking
in tongues." Or are we really inclined to regard these works as manifestos
of an ecstatic practice, as messages whose content no one understands,
not even their authors? Is it really our intention to understand and
explain the creators of these works, the artists, as charismatic mediums
(or people with mediumistic gifts) or the inadvertent illustrators of
their own clinical profiles? Let us not even consider such a thing, in
which case, however, not many options are left:

What connects the historical phenomenon of "speaking in tongues" with
what this exhibition presents as "painting in tongues"—and the only
respect in which any commonality between them can be discerned—is not
much more than the fact that both cause a lot of trouble for a certain
species of reason. Such a species is narrow-minded enough to insist that

2. In order to give the reader a sense of what sort of utterance meets the psychiatric standard
of (schizophrenic) "speaking in tongues," here are two examples from an older psychiatric
textbook: Citation 1: "Miracles are occurrences that contest, understand, and defend themselves as a fulfilling accord, suitable for day and night and thus for the heights and depths
of life, and which God thus leaves their due in his will and willing and thus gives their due
according to the value of a love, and thus leads enduring and contesting. Just as according
to God's determination we have life in order to protect fulfillment in love, in the same
way only inheritance of life coincides as really existing grace." Citation 2: "The right to

the demands it makes on thought and rationality should also be fulfilled
by the subject and its psyche, believing that things should be equally
"clara et distincta" (René Descartes), equally consistent and clear cut,
in both realms. Above all, this species of reason maintains that human
beings immediately possess, in their very existence, what every object
in the world possesses in its thinking: an identity (but only in its
thinking—as a concept—and not in the being of the objects themselves,
as maintained by this species of reason, which takes its own conditions
to be those of the world).

And thus one is very much justified in wondering if the phenomenon
of "speaking/painting in tongues"—or what comes to light in it—is not
actually all that bizarre and astonishing, but that the perspective from
which it appears that way is questionable: the shallow and reasonable
belief in the unity of the person and its identity as "objective conditions" of existence.

What evidence might be presented to suggest that the precarious and
incoherent personality usually associated with speaking in tongues is
by no means the exotic phenomenon it appears to be in this particular
historical manifestation? Conversely, what objections could be made to
this construct of the "unity of the person," its "identity," which is
every bit as misleading as it is practical and reasonable?

The answer is: quite a lot. The problem, however, is that, insofar
as that material is scientific and psychological in nature, this is not
the appropriate place to present it. I therefore propose to make do by
using a series of anecdotal arguments to paraphrase what cannot be set
forth here with scientific rigor. My intention is not to prove anything
conclusively, but only to encourage reservations concerning much that is
considered all too certain.

exist of a human being whom enthusiasm has caused to degenerate to the point of nuanced
attitudes." Hans W. Gruhle, ed., Lehrbuch der Nerven- und Geisteskrankheiten
(Halle, Germany: Marhold, 1952), 653.

3.   Gerhard Kloos, Grundriß der Psychiatrie und Neurologie: Mit besonderer Berücksichtigung der
Untersuchungstechnik (Munich, Germany: Müller & Steinicke, 1960), 399. See also George Barton
Cutten, Speaking with Tongues: Historically and Psychologically Considered (New Haven,
Connecticut: Yale University Press, 1927).

The indisputable fascination in the "multiplicity of tongues," as thematized by this exhibition, is strikingly similar to the fascination that so-called multiple-personality disorder has held for many people for a number of years. Even if the diagnosis itself has since turned out to be the very combination of hysteria and hoax that someone familiar with the subject could easily see in it from the beginning, the sensation around it only raises the question yet again of the whence and why of this fondness for the theme of "the subject's precarious identity" as manifested by the popular success of this diagnostic construct and also, indeed, by the fact that a phenomenon as remote—and not only in a historical sense —as that of speaking in tongues is drawn upon to characterize a contemporary artistic practice.

Framed as a thesis: an observer is never more stupefied, more fascinated, and more astonished than when he is confronted with something that is native and near to him but which he has completely repressed. In this context, astonishment is a defense mechanism, a dissimulating trick, which the observer uses to convince himself that he is completely free of this thing that forms the object of his fascinated amazement. And just as the observer's alienation vis-à-vis an object proves not (in this case) the distance of the object but the observer's denied closeness to it, in the same way the degree of his astonishment does not reflect the greatness of his surprise, much less the novelty of its subject, but rather indicates the extent to which that subject has been repressed.

It is not hard to guess what this strategy of alienation is all about. After all, since Michel Foucault,[4] we recognize how much the astonishment and the animated discourse of the sane, confronted with the strange behavior of those who are ostensibly "crazy," serves as an outlet for their own problems. It allows them, albeit indirectly, to address at least

4. See Michel Foucault, Madness and Civilization: A History of Insanity in the Age of Reason, trans. Richard Howard (New York: Vintage Books, 1965).

5. Michel de Montaigne, "On the Inconstancy of Our Actions," in The Complete Essays, trans. and ed. M. A. Screech (London: Penguin Books, 2003), 380 (II:1).

some portion of their own identical anomalies and contradictions vicariously, while at the same time showing, or more precisely maintaining—with the so-very-reasonable way they speak about them—that they are free of them.

The question is, then, what difficult personal experiences is the public addressing when it turns with such interest—with this blend of fascination and alienation—to phenomena such as speaking in tongues or multiple-personality disorder?

First, however, a few citations from older literature, which may help to show that it truly takes a certain amount of ignorance or repression to regard the precarious unity of person—for which the phenomena under discussion are representative—as something outrageous and unheard of, much less entirely new (and which illustrate that already in earlier times the reality of this unity was not as self-evident as perceived often enough still today):

Did not Michel de Montaigne in 1580 already believe that "there is as much difference between us and ourselves as there is between us and other people?"[5]

Did not Denis Diderot in 1774 already meet a man of whom he said, "Nothing is less like him than himself?"[6]

What about Arthur Rimbaud in 1871 with his dictum that "I is someone else" and a biography that implies the same proposition?[7]

Did not Charles Morton Cooley—who coined the term "looking-glass self" to characterize the phenomenon—in 1902 already describe how the subject is not only made up of what it is by itself and for itself, but always also of what it is for others, and therefore just how different it can be from itself?[8]

Did not Fernando Pessoa's own life already give him occasion to

6. Denis Diderot, Rameau's Nephew, in Rameau's Nephew and D'Alembert's Dream, trans. L. W. Tancock (Harmondsworth, England: Penguin Books, 1966), 34.

7. Arthur Rimbaud, letter to Paul Demeny, 15 May 1871, in Rimbaud Complete, trans. and ed. Wyatt Mason, vol. 2, I Promise to Be Good: The Letters of Arthur Rimbaud (New York: The Modern Library, 2003), 31.

8. Charles Horton Cooley, Human Nature and the Social Order (New York: Scribner, 1902), especially 179–85.

observe in 1932, "Each of us is various, many people, a prolixity
of selves"?[9]
It is hardly necessary to go on and point to Dr. Jekyll and Mr. Hyde and
the doppelgänger topos—already so widespread among the Romantics—to recognize that if anything has recently become precarious about the "unity
of [the] person," it must be the belief in it and not that unity itself.

On the other hand—and this brings us back to the question above—it
must be assumed that this belief in the subject's unity and personal
identity could not have become so uncertain unless real events and con-
crete experiences had actually caused those things to become precarious.
What events and experiences might those be? Here, too, are mere suggestions:

When we see, for example, how common it has become that people need
other, professional "auxiliary-egos" (Freud) to assist in the maintenance
and upkeep of their own and delegate portions of their psychological
life to "servo-existences" who specialize in providing that assistance—
the therapist, the wellness trainer, the analyst, the Ayurvedic guide,
the spiritual advisor, the mental coach, the beauty advisor, the divorce
mediator, the yoga teacher, etc.—and thus how, in the name of optimal
self-realization, individuals continually open new "ego subsidiaries"
of this kind and thus, as it were, outsource more and more of their
ego's functions;

When we see, for example, how much more often people today are touched
by events in fictional or distant worlds—through television, film, and
other media—than they are by what actually happens in their own lives,
and how willingly they surrender themselves to these mediated serial
experiences of captivation, which the entertainment industry serves up
to them; in short, when we see how amusing and entertaining people find
it to be relieved of their selves;

---

9. Fernando Pessoa, The Book of Disquiet, trans. Alfred Mac Adam (New York: Pantheon Books, 1991),
15 (note of 30 December 1932).

When we see, for example, how common it has become for people to
appear, by dint of their clothing, under every conceivable name—"Diesel,"
"Gucci," "Nike," "Prada," etc.—but never their own, and how with every
new seasonal act of self-labeling they take new pains to accomplish something that used to be regarded as having been settled once and for all
by their christening, that is, identifiability and group membership,
(social) identity;

When we see, for example, how freely and joyfully people use their
cell phones to regress to that state of permanent and ubiquitous presence
and connection that was once their intrauterine destiny, when they were
still attached to the umbilical cord; and how, with this communicative
chaining and connection—made possible by the telephone freed of its cord—
they seek, as it were, to abolish the act with which all individuation
begins: cutting the cord;

etc., etc.;

Then we will surely have reason enough to affirm that in their empirical
existence, people have actually strayed quite far from that norm that still
concerns them so terribly, and which the dictum of the unity of person
presents as their duty: the sovereignty of the "I" and individual identity.

Before we find this too unfortunate, however, we should consider how
much of what we mean by "unity of person" or "personal identity"—which
has been and continues to be regarded as a human duty—serves no higher
purpose than to stabilize interpersonal relations and render individual
behavior predictable for the greater good of society. The fact that what
the subject called "I" yesterday is the same thing it calls "I" today
and will call "I" tomorrow (identity); and the fact that, when it brushes
its teeth, the one who brushes and the one whose teeth are brushed are
one and the same (unity of person)—this may very well make the subject's

existence easier too, especially in its practical interactions with itself. Certainly it considerably diminishes the variety in the subject's
experiences of itself and the world and with it their entertainment
function. Above all, however, because it makes the subject's behavior
so calculable and predictable, it renders its existence much easier to
manage for everyone who has demands upon it, including spouse, employer,
state, colleague, landlord, subordinate, etc.

110   In view of this consideration, one should no longer find the suspicion
so disturbing that, in losing its identity, the subject may have far less
to lose than its fellow human beings and that the latter always have
greater cause than the subject to fear that loss. For, at the very least,
the loss of its identity brings tremendous variety into the subject's
life, which undoubtedly gains in entertainment value, at least in and
for itself and not infrequently—as this exhibition may help to show—for
others as well.

And so perhaps I too may be permitted to close with the words that
Gufo Reale—that strong German thinker who, alas, disappeared too early—
used to conclude his legendary tirades against so-called self-realization
and other efforts to "find oneself" and become "authentic," all of which
make depression a foregone conclusion: "Alienate yourselves and you
amuse yourselves!"[10]

POSTSCRIPT

One can look at things that way. But one can also look at things
differently and ask:

> Have there not always been periods in the history of art, periods
> described as "late" or labeled as "decadence," in which an artistic
> skill had become so sublime that it ceased to regard anything other

---

10. From a speech by Gufo Reale. Last traces of this thinker may be found in the journal Inter-
     funktionen (Cologne, Germany), no. 9 (1973): 152, and no. 10 (1974): 104; and in the
     exhibition catalogue Sigmar Polke: Werke aus der Sammlung Froehlich, Museum für Neue Kunst,
     Karlsruhe, Germany (Ostfildern-Ruit, Germany: Hatje Cantz, 2000), 34.

than itself as worthy of representation, so that artworks became
works of artistry?
in which the number of creative forms had become so finite that it
was only possible to fashion a new one by repeating and mixing them,
so that images increasingly became images of images?
in which searching had been lost in its experiences of finding, so
that the great search for searching became the order of the day and
in the process, searching became a gesture (mimicry)?

And is it perhaps the case that what is displayed by "appropriation
art" and "sampling" and "remix" and "medley" and "painting in tongues"
and Gerhard Richter (who is often mentioned in connection with this kind
of painting) is, once again, an aesthetics of decadence? The triumph of
versatility, citation, variation, and combination over stubbornness,
assertion, destruction, and creation, the triumph of artistic refinement
over "creative fury"?

That need not necessarily be true to be worth thinking about.

And what if it were true and prompted reservations about this art?
Then we would have failed to appreciate the art within this art and reduced
it to what—in this art as in every other—is the symptomology of a time.

Translated by James Gussen